The
LAST TSAR

FRONTISPIECE Nicholas and Alexandra.

Virginia Cowles

The LAST TSAR

G. P. Putnam's Sons · New York

To Eliane and Bob d'Espous
and
Villeperdue

First American Edition, 1977

Designed by Craig Dodd
for George Weidenfeld and Nicolson Ltd
11 St John's Hill, London SW11
House editor Esther Jagger

Library of Congress Catalog Card Number: 77–147
SBN: 399–11974–4

Printed in Great Britain by
Morrison & Gibb Ltd., London and Edinburgh

Contents

1

In the Shadow of the Throne

Although Nicholas II could not know that Fate had marked him down as the last Tsar of Russia, he was haunted by a sense of doom that followed him all his life. This was partly caused by superstition. His birthday fell on 6 May, the feast of Job, and he identified every disappointment he experienced with the words of the prophet. 'Hardly do I have a fear than it is realized, and all the misfortune that I dread falls upon me.'

Nicholas often looked back nostalgically to the undemanding days of his childhood. In 1876, when he was eight years old, he was a blessed nonentity. His grandfather, Alexander II, was Emperor of Russia, and his father, the Tsarevich Alexander, was heir to the throne. Nicholas was too young and too far removed from power to excite much interest and was perfectly content with the placid routine of his spacious, white-washed nurseries. The fact that he lived in the Anitchkov Palace, a massive building on the Nevsky Prospect of St Petersburg, was of no interest to him at this time.

Nicholas's inseparable companion was his brother George, two and a half years his junior. His sister Xenia was still a baby and Michael and Olga were not yet born. The children were brought up in a pretence of spartan simplicity. They ate off thick, unbreakable crockery and slept on narrow camp beds. Yet their playrooms were a fairyland of extravagance: wooden hills with tracks and little wheeled trolleys; a fully equipped gymnasium; a merry-go-round; a toy railway with switches and signal posts; a mechanical orchestra with self-playing piano; a doll's house with a real cooking stove and a parlour where the food could be sampled.

Nicholas and George shared the same nannies and tutors. Their mother, the Grand Duchess Marie Fedorovna, had been born Princess Dagmar, a daughter of King Christian IX of Denmark. She was not a beauty like her sister, Alexandra, who was married to the Prince of Wales; but she loved clothes and jewellery and was ready to dance all night which endeared her to Russian society. The gaiety of her life prevented her from spending much time with her sons but she had firm ideas about their education. Since she was not a clever woman herself she stood in awe of learning and believed that children's minds should not be too highly taxed; she even had a theory that excessive study could bring on brain fever. Nevertheless she considered it essential that her children should be able to converse fluently in several languages, and made a point of engaging English nannies and French and German governesses who would pass on their mother tongues as effortlessly as possible. Later the boys had an English tutor, Mr Heath, who taught them geography and European history and did his best to turn them into English

OPPOSITE Grand Duchess Marie Fedorovna with the two-year-old Nicholas.

Nicholas aged about ten, with his sister Xenia,
his brother George and his parents.

gentlemen; and a Russian master, Danilich, who grounded them in Russian history. The Romanov dynasty, the boys learned, had sprung into being in 1613 in the angry glare of 'The Troubled Times'. This modest phrase was used to describe the utter chaos that marked the end of the Rurik line at the close of the sixteenth century. The Church had taken upon itself the task of finding a new ruler, finally settling upon a relatively unknown boy, sixteen-year-old Michael Romanov. Although Michael did not possess a drop of royal blood his father, the Patriarch Philaret, had the right ecclesiastical connections and could even boast an aunt, Anastasia Romanova, who had had the temerity to marry Ivan the Terrible.

When the crown was set on Michael's head his kingdom, which consisted mainly of Muscovy, was invaded from the west by Swedes and Poles, and from the east by marauding bands of Cossacks and Crim Tartars. Not until his thirty-year reign was almost at an end could he claim to have eliminated his enemies and restored the kingdom to order.

Whether at peace or at war, Muscovy was not regarded as a civilized state by the countries of Europe. Although the Russ tribes had been converted to Christianity in the tenth century by Byzantine missionaries, the Mongol invasion that took place 250 years later had introduced autocracy in its most sadistic form, even managing to twist the peoples' faith in one God into an Asiatic fear of the supernatural.

Michael was a good ruler; but the Romanovs who followed him were savage and perverse and notorious for their bad manners. The boyars copied their tsars and shocked Europe with their uncouth ways. Indeed, the tsars' ambassadors to the west incurred such disapproval by their rowdy behaviour that the Austrian Emperor refused to give the usual golden chains and portraits 'to such worthless dogs'; Christian IV of Denmark said: 'If these people come again we must build them a pig sty for nobody can live in any house that they have occupied till six months afterwards because of the stench they have left behind them.' Drunkenness, licentiousness and dirt were minor crimes. The early Romanovs were notorious for fiendish tortures; when at last they were prevailed upon to abandon these medieval practices they introduced the whip and the knout as a sign of enlightenment. As a dynasty the Romanovs had a tendency to murder their kith and kin. Peter the Great tortured to death his own son; Catherine the Great encouraged her lover to kill her husband; and Alexander I, an intellectual and a mystic, revered by many as a saintly man, acquiesced in the assassination of his father.

No doubt the Russian tutor of the Grand Dukes slid over these unpleasantries and emphasized instead the passion of all Romanovs for glory through expansion. Peter the Great had wrested thousands of square miles from the Swedish Empire while Catherine the Great had annexed the Crimea, the Ukraine and three-quarters of Poland and Courland. Two more tsars, including Nicholas's grandfather, had added great tracts of land in Central Asia. The Romanov domain that Nicholas would inherit now sprawled across the world from the Baltic Sea to China, and contained over 120 nationalities, ranging from Finns to Mongolians, from Poles to Tartars, from Uzbeks to Armenians.

Nicholas was a good-natured, lethargic boy whose uninquiring mind worried his tutors; George, on the other hand, was spirited and imaginative, and despite being younger soon managed to establish his mastery. Nicholas was so fascinated by everything George said or did that he copied his jokes on to bits of paper and filed them away in a box. Years later someone heard Nicholas laughing behind closed doors and entered to find him re-reading his brother's witticisms.

The children usually lunched with their parents, and George frequently goaded Nicholas into such unruly acts as throwing bits of bread across the table. Although the nannies were indignant, the Grand Ducal couple never seemed to notice. George grew bolder and once he committed an enormity. When the two boys were attending a grown-up tea party given by their mother, he suddenly thrust out his leg and tripped up the butler who was carrying a large tray. No one knows what punishment was meted out on this occasion; but the truth was that, although the Grand Duchess was strict with her daughters, she could never bring herself to punish the boys. Sometimes she allowed them to come into her bedroom when she was dressing for dinner and made them feel important by asking them which dress would be the prettiest for her to wear. They sat on the floor and watched her putting ropes of pearls around her neck while her maid tried to do her hair.

If the boys were fond of their mother, they worshipped the resplendently uniformed giant who was their father. The Tsarevich could tie an iron poker in knots and tear a pack of cards in two. Since he was a professional soldier he spent most of his time in St Petersburg where his Guards Regiment was stationed. But on holidays he frequently took his family to the palace at Tsarskoe Selo, fourteen miles away, or to Peterhof, the famous royal residence on the Gulf of Finland, built by Peter the Great to rival Versailles.

Once a year they travelled from Peterhof to Kronstadt and boarded the imperial yacht for Denmark to stay with their grandfather, King Christian IX, at Fredensborg. Twenty railway carriages were needed to carry their luggage to the boat, and over a hundred servants travelled with them. Guests at the other end often included King George and Queen Olga of Greece and their seven lively children; the Princess of Wales and her family; the Duke and Duchess of Cumberland; and any number of relations from Sweden and Austria, all with nannies and offspring. The children adored the visit as they camped in the park and were free from supervision. Nicholas and George, for instance, shared a hut in the rose garden and spent their days searching for tadpoles in the muddy ponds, climbing trees and stealing apples, and organizing all sorts of competitive jumps and races.

For Nicholas, an even more glorious treat than Denmark was to accompany his father to Spala, a hunting lodge in Russian-occupied Poland,

Nicholas and George, a photograph taken
at Livadia in 1886.

where they shot bison and wild pig and stalked deer. Once Alexander took him on a never-to-be-forgotten journey to watch manoeuvres at Krasnoe Selo. At night he slept in a tent and in the day looked through field glasses at the troops deploying on the fields below.

The grandest military occasions, of course, were the reviews at which the Tsar took the salute. Nicholas was greatly in awe of the tall, imposing man who was his grandfather. This was not surprising because even foreign representatives were nervous in his presence. He received diplomats in Peter the Great's hall in the Winter Palace and always sat on Peter's throne. The room was magnificent with jasper columns and walls hung with red velvet and magnificent two-headed eagles. 'He was wonderfully handsome even in old age,' wrote a British diplomat, 'with a most commanding manner and an air of freezing *hauteur*. When addressing junior members of the Diplomatic body, there was something in his voice and a look in his eyes reminiscent of the Grand Mogul addressing an earth worm.'[1] The freezing *hauteur* was misleading, for Alexander II cared deeply for his people and had introduced more reforms than any other tsar. His greatest single contribution was the emancipation of the serfs, for which he was known as 'the Tsar-Liberator'.

The Emperor's son, the Tsarevich Alexander – Nicholas's father – was often at loggerheads with his parents, for like most soldiers he was deeply conservative. Furthermore he was under the influence of his tutor, Constantine Pobedonostsvev, who was soon to become Procurator of the Holy Synod. Although he was a brilliant teacher, he was so reactionary that he was

Constantine Pobedonostsvev, the 'Black Tsar'.

known as the 'Black Tsar'. He indoctrinated young Alexander with a contempt ıor representative government as 'the greatest illustration of human delusion'; for all reforms as 'cheap and shallow ecstacies'; a Press as an 'instrument of mass corruption'. Above all he impressed upon him the supreme importance of accepting autocracy and orthodoxy as Russia's double-headed eagle; the tsar's will was inviolate, because the tsar was chosen by God.

When the Emperor's reforms suddenly gave rise to a violent creed known as Nihilism, Pobedonostsvev's warnings commanded new attention. The Nihilists advocated wholesale destruction in order to create a vacuum. The theory was that something better – nobody knew what – was bound to fill the void. The relentless pressure of the attacks finally led the Tsar to rescind some of his concessions; and young Alexander began to look upon Pobedonostsvev not only as a tutor but as a prophet.

The Grand Duke Alexander had not become heir-apparent until he was twenty-one, when his elder brother – another Nicholas – contracted meningitis and died. On his deathbed Nicholas bequeathed to Alexander not only the promise of a throne but a flesh and blood fiancée. Princess Dagmar of Denmark was betrothed to Nicholas, and when Alexander knelt beside him, Nicholas took her hand and placed it in Alexander's massive fist. The subsequent marriage was surprisingly successful, for although the new Tsarevich hated society and had little in common with his butterfly wife, he fell beneath her charm and became the first Romanov to be both a good husband and a good father.

Until the future Nicholas II was eight years old, his life was uneventful. Then suddenly, in 1876, he found himself surrounded by people clamouring for war. Overnight the red, white and blue Slavonic flag fluttered from hundreds of buildings, and elderly ladies who were members of the Empress's court stood on icy street corners jingling money boxes in aid of poor little Serbia.

The truth was that all devout Russians cherished a secret dream to free the Balkan Slavs from their Turkish masters and to march to Constantinople and restore Santa Sophia as the fount of Orthodoxy. Indeed Russia had fought six wars against Turkey on religious grounds, and now Serbia, a small, independent country, was snatching the torch from Russian hands. Angered because Turkish landlords in Herzegovina had maltreated Serbian peasants, the Serbs on their own initiative had declared war on the Sultan. The smouldering hatred for Islam, buried in Russian breasts, suddenly burst into flame. The Emperor was appalled by the frenzied clamour to support Serbia. He knew that talk of a religious crusade, genuine enough with priests and old ladies, was only a facade for the secret ambitions of his military imperialists. Ever since Bismarck had united Germany and crowned the King of Prussia as German Emperor in 1871, Russian chiefs of staff had been searching jealously for a chance to even the score. The Tsar's admirals wanted to open the Turkish Straits, and the Tsar's generals wanted to establish a Greater Serbia or Bulgaria as a Russian satellite.

Since Alexander II was convinced that neither of these goals would be tolerated by the Great Powers he did his best to lower the temperature. He was spectacularly unsuccessful, for he could not even control his own family. The deeply religious Empress became President of the Red Cross and fitted out hospital trains for the Balkans at her own expense; and she took under her protection three of the daughters of the King of Montenegro and sent them to the fashionable Smolny Institute in St Petersburg, while the heir-apparent encouraged men of the Guards Regiment to volunteer for service in Serbia, promising to reinstate them upon their return.

Nicholas did not know until he was an adult that his grandfather's inability to command the allegiance of his wife and son was the result of the Tsar's love affair with Catherine Dolgorouky, a beautiful twenty-seven-year-old Russian princess young enough to be his daughter. Catherine had borne the Emperor three children and he had given the scandal a new twist by allowing his bastard offspring to use his patronym. Although the Empress quietly accepted her husband's behaviour, turning to the priests for solace, her four sons were outraged. They made their hostility plain by refusing to follow the Tsar's lead and pursuing instead their own inclinations.

In the end, the weight of public opinion forced Alexander II to lead his country into war. Young Nicholas was allowed to accompany his mother to the station to see his father off. Bands were playing and the platform swarmed with officers in brilliant uniforms. The Grand Duchess said goodbye in a flood of tears which added to the general excitement.

In distant London Queen Victoria was so agitated about the supine attitude of her government to what she called 'Russian aggression' that she threatened to abdicate. 'If England is to kiss Russia's feet', she wrote to her Prime Minister, 'the Queen will not be a party to the humiliation of England and would lay down her crown.' At the same time she sent a memorandum to her Cabinet emphasizing that the crisis was not a question of 'upholding Turkey'; 'It is the question of Russian or British supremacy in the world!' What the Queen wanted was a firm declaration of intent, 'clearly explained to the other powers ... that we cannot allow the Russians to occupy Constantinople.'[2]

Meanwhile the Russian army was running into trouble. The High Command decided to bombard the heavily fortified Turkish positions at Plevna, then send in the infantry to take the strongholds at the point of a bayonet. The military textbooks taught that although the first, second and third waves of men might go down, the fourth, fifth and sixth would be successful. This reckoning, however, belonged to an earlier decade, for the Turks were equipped with a Krupp field gun, never before seen in action. They were breach-loading guns made of steel, far superior to the bronze pieces of their opponents. Even their side-arms, Peabody-Martini repeating rifles made in Providence, Rhode Island, were more effective than the old French rifles used against them.

During two days of hideous slaughter, the Turks mowed down 25,000 Russians who failed to gain an inch of ground. Veteran war correspondents were amazed by the advance in artillery fire-power and wrote that undoubtedly they were witnessing set battles that marked the end of an era. Tactics that relied mainly on men against metal, they pointed out, would not be tolerated in future planning. Yet thirty-five years later, in 1914, these unacceptable tactics were accepted as the order of the day.

Eventually, superiority in numbers made itself felt and the Russians advanced to Adrianople, only sixty miles from Constantinople. At that point the British government made its attitude plain by sending six warships through the Dardanelles. The threat was real, and, just as the Tsar had predicted, the Russians were obliged to forget Constantinople and to go home. At the Peace Conference, held in Berlin, Russia met further rebuffs. The Great Powers objected to 'Greater Bulgaria', which they correctly envisaged as a Russian satellite, and insisted that the country must be divided in two, one half remaining under Turkish rule.

If the Russians had fought the war for the reasons they professed – to free the Christian Slavs from Turkish rule – they would have been satisfied with the results. The Tsar's troops had, in fact, all but pushed the Turks out of Europe and recovered that part of Bessarabia lost after the Crimean War. Furthermore, they had extended their Asian territory by thousands of miles by adding Kars, Batuum and Ardaghan. On the other hand, Russia once again had been denied access to the Mediterranean which she had hoped to reach through the Bulgarian back door. And that, as Disraeli crowed to Queen Victoria, 'was the real object of the late war'. The Russian Foreign Minister says, he added happily, that 'Russia has sacrificed 100,000 picked soldiers and £100,000 [then a vast sum] of money for nothing.'

Nicholas's grandfather looked old and ill. Although Alexander II had tried hard to keep his country out of war, he was blamed for every reverse; before long public anguish gave way, as it always seemed to do in Russia, to a new wave of violence. This time the youthful assassins walked into the offices of governors and police chiefs, shot them dead, and gave themselves up to arrest.

One of the terrorists, Vera Zasulich, sought an interview with General Trepov, Chief of the St Petersburg Police, pulled out a revolver and shot him twice. Her aim was so bad that he did not die but was seriously wounded. However, at her trial her lawyer painted such a romantic picture of a pure young girl in search of social justice that the jury acquitted her. The great writer, Tolstoy, was horrified. 'This Zasulich business is no joking matter', he wrote to a friend, '. . . the Slavophil madness was the precursor of war, and I am inclined to think that this madness is the precursor of revolution. . . .'[3] The revolution was still a long way off, but the madness continued.

Although Nicholas and George were supposed to be insulated from the ugly happenings of the outside world, very little remained hidden from them.

17

Tsar Alexander II, Nicholas's grandfather – the Tsar-Liberator.

The servants were always overflowing with gossip and even the tutors found it impossible to remain impassive when some horrific event took place. But the most willing informer was Nicholas's cousin and contemporary, the young Grand Duke Alexander Mikhailovich, known as 'Sandro', who later married Nicholas's sister, Xenia.

Sandro was a mine of information since his parents talked freely in front of him. He explained that a group of terrorists known as Will of the People had taken an oath to kill the Tsar. Experimenting with explosives developed in the recent war, they planted a charge underneath the imperial train when it stopped in Moscow *en route* for St Petersburg. However, they mistook the baggage car for the Tsar's quarters and Alexander was safely inside the Kremlin when the explosion blew three coaches off the track. When the Emperor was told what had happened he exclaimed bitterly: 'Am I such a wild beast that they must hound me to death?'

Next the terrorists managed to slip an explosives expert into the work force that was carrying out repairs in the basement of the Winter Palace. This man mined an area directly below the dining-room, but once again the plan failed. Dinner was postponed half an hour because a foreign guest was late, and the explosion occurred while the Tsar was still in the drawing-room. The only fatal casualties were among a regiment of Swiss Guards who used a downstairs room as a mess.

'To say that we live in a besieged fortress', Sandro wrote many years later, 'would be using a poor simile. In war time one knew one's friends and enemies. We never did. The butler serving morning coffee might have been in the employ of the Nihilists for all we knew ... a potential bearer of an infernal machine.'[4] People were so frightened of the relentless campaign that when the Tsar attended an Opera Gala before Christmas, the house was half empty. The Tsarina was never with him now, since she was gravely ill. She lay in her bedroom, surrounded by oxygen cylinders, preparing herself for the next world. Her death came a few weeks after the attack on the Winter Palace.

A month later Alexander II proclaimed the period of mourning at an end and took Catherine as his morganatic wife, giving her the title of Princess Yurievskaya. He told his sister that because he did not know from day to day when his end would come he was forced to act hastily. Nevertheless he decided to return to the liberal ideas that had animated the first years of his reign. He appointed a new Prime Minister and signed an historic document announcing that representatives of local government would be invited to join a new Council of State – Russia's first step towards parliamentary government. It was agreed that the document would be released to the press on Monday morning. But on Sunday, when Alexander II was on his way home from Michael's Riding School where he had been attending the weekly parade, he was attacked once again. The four magnificent Orlov trotters pulling his carriage moved so fast over the hard-packed snow that his Cossack Guard broke into a gallop to keep pace with him. Following were two sleighs filled with police officers and attendants.

As the imperial coach passed an intersection a young man ran to the corner and threw a parcel in front of the horses. The explosion could be heard at the Winter Palace. When the smoke thinned two of the Cossacks and three of the horses were lying in a river of blood but Alexander jumped out unhurt. The

An artist's impression of the assassination of Alexander II in 1881.

police, meanwhile, had leapt from their sledges and caught the assassin. People came running from all directions. 'Thank God your Majesty is safe,' said one of the guards. 'Rather too early to thank God,' shouted a voice from the pavement. A second young man raised his arm and threw what looked like a snowball at the Tsar's feet.

The second explosion was so loud that it shook the quay from end to end. Smoke and snow blinded the crowd. When it cleared, more than twenty people were lying on the ground, their blood staining the white road. The Emperor half lay, half sat, his back to the canal railings. His face was streaming with blood, his abdomen was torn open, his legs shattered. 'Quickly. Home to the palace to die,' he murmured, and lost consciousness.

Everyone seemed to know what had happened long before the sledge entered the palace gates. 'We ... started a mad race toward the Winter Palace,' wrote the young Grand Duke Alexander Mikhailovich, 'passing on our way the Preobrazhensky Regiment of the Guards doubling in the same direction with fixed bayonets. Thousands of people were already surrounding the palace ... there was no need to ask questions; large drops of black blood showed us the way up the marble steps and then across a corridor into the Emperor's study.'[5]

It was remarkable how quickly members of the Romanov family reached the palace. The heir to the throne and the Grand Duchess Marie Fedorovna were already there; so was Nicholas, dressed in his Sunday sailor suit. One by one the relations crowded into the room and stood in horrified groups as the doctors hovered futilely over the dying man and the priests whispered last rites. Suddenly Princess Yurievskaya burst in, in a negligee. Apparently she had been changing her clothes for the afternoon promenade. She fell flat on the couch over the body of the Tsar, screaming: 'Sasha! Sasha!' A few minutes later the Emperor was dead and the princess dropped on the floor 'like a felled tree'.

Nicholas was thirteen years old when he became Tsarevich. Under normal circumstances he would have been obliged to live a semi-official life, accompanying his father to a good many public functions. Instead, the police begged the new Tsar to leave the capital. Not only was it impossible to guard the Winter Palace, which stretched a quarter of a mile along the Neva, but every journey through the streets of St Petersburg was fraught with danger.

Alexander III had always loathed cities and social gatherings, so he readily assented and moved his family to Gatchina, forty miles away. This vast palace, the home of Paul I, had 600 bedrooms. It was surrounded by a moat and lay in a large park complete with forests and lakes and thousands of acres of farmland. Its isolation made it easier to protect than any other palace, and every precaution was taken. An army of 10,000 men was moved on to the property and dozens of small camps were set up. Furthermore the house and park were ringed with sentries, stationed at twenty-five-metre intervals and changed every few hours.

General Tcherevin, head of the secret police and a friend of the Emperor, took his duties so seriously that he lived at Gatchina six months of the year. The food put before the Emperor was prepared by a French chef, under constant police supervision. On the rare occasions when Alexander left his fastness and visited the capital, he rode to the station in an armour-plated carriage which had once belonged to Napoleon III. The vehicle was so heavy that the horses who pulled it soon died of exhaustion.

The new Tsar had none of his father's liberal leanings, and in his accession manifesto announced that he would rule 'with faith in the power and truth of the Absolutism we are called upon to defend'. Leaving no room for doubt, he went on to say: 'We are determined to strengthen the State against any attempt to weaken Our power, and this we do for the benefit of Our people.' He dismissed the dead Emperor's Prime Minister and tore up the document paving the way for representative government. Thousands of suspects were rounded up and sent to Siberia, censorship was tightened, university studies were curtailed, and once again trials took place in secret.

Gradually all the major revolutionary organizations were broken up; yet individual terrorists continued to commit acts of terrorism which gave the public a false sense of their strength. In 1882 General Strenikov, Public

OVERLEAF The palace at Gatchina.

Prosecutor of Kiev, was assassinated while sitting on the boulevard in Odessa. A few weeks later a mine was discovered in the Kremlin where preparations were under way for the Tsar's coronation. At Easter the head of the Moscow police received a basketful of artificial eggs, several of which were charged with dynamite. In 1883 General Sudeiken, Chief of the St Petersburg Police, was found battered to death in his flat. These incidents did not soothe the imperial nerves. 'The slightest rumours were believed', declared a Court official, 'Assassins masked in Court livery, bombs hidden in the park, threatening letters found on the table – the most ordinary happenings were magnified to tales of horror.'

Alexander III had not inherited his father's icy composure and the daily tension often put his nerves on edge. He was in the habit of taking a nap in his study after lunch, and one day the Empress Marie heard a pistol shot. With her heart beating wildly she ran into the room and found the Tsar sitting, half-dazed, on the edge of his sofa, a gun in his hand. At his feet lay his *aide-de-camp* with a bullet through his head. Alexander had woken up to see the man standing over him with his fingers on his throat. He had snatched his revolver from under a cushion and fired. Apparently, the *aide-de-camp* had come into the study with papers, and seeing the Emperor dozing, with a constricted look on his face, had attempted to unhook his military collar.

Fear, however, played no part in the lives of the children. Nicholas and George did their lessons in the morning, and in the afternoon built secret houses in the woods, took boat trips on the lake or galloped their horses across the flat fields of the home farm. Although the armed guards were a reminder of emergency, they felt an exhilarating sense of freedom in the country. Gradually thoughts of terrorists began to fade away; and by the end of the decade the terrorists themselves had been eliminated.

The children lived far more austerely at Gatchina than in St Petersburg. Alexander III was frugal to the point of miserliness, and here in the country he had time to survey every aspect of the housekeeping. Not only did he cut down on official entertaining and make stringent economies on food and wine, but he issued orders that soap and candles must be used up before they were thrown away, that table linen was not to be changed every day, and that lights were not to be left burning in empty rooms. He even decided that twenty people did not need an omelette made of a hundred eggs. Alexander's favourite food was cabbage and gruel, and although he did not inflict these dishes on his guests, visitors frequently complained that the food at Gatchina was inedible. Count Witte went even further. 'The Imperial table was always relatively poor,' he wrote, 'and the food served at the Court Marshal's board was sometimes such as to endanger health.'[6]

Once Nicholas was so hungry that he opened the gold cross given to him at his baptism and ate the beeswax inside. This was an act of blasphemy, his sister Olga explained, for 'an infinitesimal relic of the True Cross was embedded in wax'. Later he felt very ashamed of himself, but admitted that it had tasted 'immorally good'. The reason for Nicholas's hunger, however, was not a lack of food but a lack of time in which to consume it. The Empress had taken a leaf from the book of her sister, Alexandra, Princess of Wales, who boasted that meals at Buckingham Palace never took longer than one hour. The Empress went one better and laid down a fifty-minute time limit. Because the children were always the last to be served, they had only a few mouthfuls before their plates were removed.

When the Tsar lunched alone with his family he often wore the baggy Russian trousers and loose blouse of the peasant. This was part of a new campaign, 'Russia for the Russians', which stemmed from the teaching of Constantine Pobedonostsev, now the Procurator of the Holy Synod. The 'Black Tsar' spent half the year at Gatchina in the dual capacity of adviser to Alexander III and tutor to Nicholas. He preached a sort of trialism: faith not only in Autocracy and Orthodoxy but in Nationalism. This last word had a curious ring, since the huge, patchwork Russian Empire comprised dozens of races and creeds and languages. Indeed, the Tsar himself could scarcely be catalogued as a pure-bred Russian – almost every drop of blood in his veins was German. His mother was a princess of Hesse-Darmstadt, his grandmother a princess of Prussia, his great-grandmother a princess of Württemburg, and his great-great-grandmother Catherine the Great, a princess of Anhalt-Zerbst, who married a German prince of Holstein-Gottorp. Even Alexander III's wife, whom he was fond of describing as 'a Danish princess', was wholly German. Before her father ascended the throne as Christian IX of Denmark he was Prince Glücksberg of Holstein. He was invited to become king when the old Danish dynasty expired.

The meaning of Pobedonostsev's 'nationalism' was simply that all groups should allow themselves to be assimilated by Russian customs and the Orthodox religion. Obediently, Alexander III made the Russian language compulsory in Finland and the Baltic states, prohibited members of the court from using the German language and called for a new military uniform eliminating all Prussian details. Even German families who had been living in Russia since the days of Peter the Great were classified as 'foreigners' and disqualified from inheriting property.

Far worse was the treatment meted out to the Jews. They became the target of fierce pogroms and deportations unequalled until the days of Adolf Hitler. Pobedonostsev proclaimed that one third of the Jews of Russia must die, one third emigrate and one third assimilate. Alexander III gave his assent because two of the terrorists who had planned the murder of his father were Jews, and he was convinced that international Jewry was organizing a gigantic plot to end the monarchical system. He never spoke of Jews as anything but 'Yids' and managed to instil his aversion into Nicholas, often reminding the boy: 'Never forget that it was the Zhidy who crucified the Lord and spilled his blood.'

Like all Russians, Tsar Alexander III had secret ambitions to extend his country's influence, perhaps even her frontiers. What was curious about the

A caricature of Pobedonostsev, entitled 'Our Lady of Peterfhof'. He preached autocracy and contempt for democracy to both Alexander III and Nicholas.

26

new Emperor was his failure to see any connection between subversion in Russia, which he fought, and subversion in the Balkans, which he encouraged. Sovereigns who preceded him argued that revolutionary activity was an epidemic. If you encouraged it abroad you could expect it at home. Alexander III, however, barricaded the doors of Gatchina Palace and allowed his Foreign Office and his military attachés to plot the downfall of brother monarchs who stood in Russia's path.

As a result, Russian agents posing as monks flooded the monastery of Mount Athos in Greece, and more agents, dressed as ikon sellers, swarmed through Serbia. In Bulgaria, members of the public were paid to stage 'spontaneous demonstrations' and the Russian *Okhrana* (secret police) even managed to organize a minor rebellion in the army which resulted in the kidnapping of the country's royal ruler, who finally abdicated.

The reign of Alexander III became so famous for its two-tiered policies – official and unofficial – that the eleventh edition of the *Encyclopedia Britannica*, issued in the latter part of the 1880s, made special reference to it: 'The Cabinet of St Petersburg confined itself *officially* to breaking off diplomatic relations with Bulgaria and making diplomatic protests, and unofficially to giving tacit encouragement to revolutionary activity.'

Nicholas's tutors found him a disappointing pupil. He seemed to suffer from intellectual lassitude from which it was impossible to arouse him. He never asked a question or challenged a statement or pursued a subject of his own accord. 'Although he learns very well,' commented one of his teachers, 'he can never understand what he is learning.' The truth was that Nicholas begrudged every hour spent in the schoolroom and longed for an out-of-door life. He loved pitching a tent for the night and cooking his supper over a fire, and he boasted that he could walk as fast as a horse. When he was nineteen, his father delighted him by assigning him a squadron in the Hussar Guards for the annual manoeuvres at Krasnoe Selo, the great military camp outside St Petersburg.

'I am happier than I can say to have joined the army,' he wrote to his mother; 'and every day I become more and more used to camp life. Every day we drill twice – there is either target practice in the morning and battalion drill in the evening or the other way around. ... The dinners are very merry, they feed us well. After meals the officers ... play billiards, skittles, cards or dominoes.'[7]

Since terrorism had begun to wane, the imperial family moved about the capital quite freely again. The Empress took up residence in Anitchkov Palace for the season – the weeks between Christmas and Lent – while Nicholas was allowed to attend theatres and ballets whenever he liked. Nevertheless, there was always a reminder of danger. That same year, in 1887, five students at St Petersburg University were accused of conspiring to kill the Tsar. One of them was caught carrying a bomb, but none of the others had done anything but talk; yet all five were condemned to death and hanged, among them Alexander Ulyanov, an elder brother of Lenin.

OVERLEAF St Petersburg in the late nineteenth century. A view of the English Quay.

*Tsar Alexander III with the Tsarina Marie Fedorovna and her sister
the Princess of Wales (right), about 1890.*

The following year the imperial family had a much nastier shock when their train, on the way home from the Caucasus, went off the rails near the town of Borki. Two engines were pulling eleven coaches when suddenly there was a violent lurch followed by a thunderous noise as three carriages careered down the embankment.

The Emperor and Empress were having lunch in the dining car with four of their children – Nicholas, George, Xenia and Michael. Although the roof fell in and the floor buckled as the coach lurched to one side, it stayed on the track. For once the Tsar's herculean strength proved of value, for he freed himself from the broken timber and iron that was crushing him, and managed to hold up the roof so that his wife and children, nannies and servants, could crawl free. Although officials attributed the accident to the decrepitude of one of the engines which had jumped the rail, pulling the coaches behind it, no one gave a convincing explanation as to why the roof of the dining car had caved in. Public opinion whispered that a bomb had exploded on the track.

Nicholas was seldom frightened, and on this occasion his chief emotion was delight at his father's superhuman strength. Otherwise the incident seemed to make no more impression on him than the routine happenings of his student existence. Even when Alexander III did him the honour of appointing him a member of the Finance Committee, Nicholas wrote laconically in his diary: 'I was present at the sitting of the Council of State which happily lasted for only twenty minutes.' And later: 'At twelve o'clock I went to town to attend the sitting of the Council of State. I left when they began to discuss the use of Latin in schools, as it bored me to death.' Even the two instructors from the St Petersburg Military Academy failed to hold his attention. 'I had Leer this morning for half an hour and he tired me excessively.' A few days later: 'Pouzerevsky stayed with me the entire morning and bored me to the point that I nearly fell asleep.'

That same year, when the Tsar allowed Nicholas to close his school-books and commissioned him as an officer in the First Horse Battery, the boy shed his famous indifference and jumped for joy. He threw himself into army life and revelled in the *camaraderie* of the officers' mess. 'We got stewed', he wrote in his diary. 'We wallowed in the grass and drank'; 'Tasted six sorts of port and got a bit soused'; 'Felt owlish'; 'The officers carried me out.'

Amid these celebrations he found time to carry on a flirtation with a charming seventeen-year-old ballet dancer – Mathilde Kschessinska – who much later became the prima ballerina of the Maryinsky; many years later she married Nicholas's cousin, the Grand Duke Andrei Vladimirovich. That autumn, however, Nicholas was forced to bid Mathilde goodbye when his father sent him and his brother George on a trip to Egypt, India and Japan. He was accompanied by his cousin, Prince George of Greece, and three young Russian noblemen. They travelled on Russian warships and at every stop were greeted by high officials. The Tsarevich found the adventure excessively dull. 'My trip is senseless', he told his brother-in-law, Sandro,

*The ballerina Mathilde Kschessinska, Nicholas's
mistress before his marriage.*

when they met in Colombo. 'Palaces and generals are the same the world over
and that is all I am permitted to see. I could just as well have stayed at home.'[8]

Japan, however, provided excitement, although not of a particularly
welcome nature. Here Nicholas was almost murdered. It happened when the
royal visitors reached Ossu, near Kyoto, and rode through the town in a
rickshaw.

We passed through a narrow street [wrote Prince George] decorated with flags and
filled with crowds of people on both sides of the thoroughfare. I was looking toward
the left when I suddenly heard something like a shriek in front of me, and saw a
policeman hitting Nicky a blow on the head with his sword, which he held with both
hands. Nicky jumped out of the cart, and the man ran after him, Nicky with the blood
streaming down his face. When I saw this, I too jumped out with my stick in my hand
and ran after the man who was about fifteen paces in front of me. Nicky ran into a
shop but came out immediately, which enabled the man to overtake him; but I thank
God that I was there the same moment and while the policeman still had the sword
high in the air I gave him a blow straight on the head, a blow so hard that he probably
had never experienced a similar one before. He now turned against me but fainted
and fell on the ground; then two of our rickshaw pullers appeared on the scene; one
got hold of his legs, while the other took the sword and gave him a wound in the back
of the head. . . .[9]

When the news of the attack reached Europe newspapers jumped to the
conclusion that the policeman was Nihilist. After an investigation, however,
it was revealed that the man was a religious fanatic, enraged at some
imaginary breach of etiquette on the part of the visitors.

Nicholas cut his trip short and returned to Russia, his head still in

Nicholas in military uniform. Although indifferent to state affairs,
as a young man he became a successful army officer.

bandages. He never forgave the Japanese, and from then on always referred
to them as 'monkeys'. Meanwhile his brother George was the victim of
something even more pernicious than an unsuccessful murder attempt.
George began to run a fever and cough up blood. The diagnosis was
tuberculosis, and the recommended cure the mountain air of the Caucasus.
George spent ten lonely years struggling against the disease which finally
caused his death.

Nicholas was a good soldier and in 1892 became head of a battalion in the
famous Preobrazhensky Regiment, with the rank of colonel. Although the
Tsar was proud of his son's success, he was disturbed by the Tsarevich's
indifference to state affairs. Nicholas admitted that he hated controversial
issues since he could always see 'two sides to a question'. Furthermore there
ran through his deeply religious nature a fatalist streak that made him accept
every happening – no matter how disappointing – as inevitable. 'God's Will
be done', was his only comment. At the same time, nothing frightened him
more than the thought that one day he would be called upon to make
decisions as his father did. But Alexander III was only forty-seven years old
in 1892, and Nicholas found no difficulty in putting the alarming prospect
out of his mind.

Although Alexander III was flattered by Nicholas's hero worship, the boy
never seemed to grow up. When Serge Witte, the Tsar's Minister of
Communications, suggested that the twenty-four-year-old Tsarevich should
be made chairman of the committee supervising the building of the Trans-
Siberian railway, which was about to be started, the Emperor looked at him
in astonishment. 'Do you know what you are asking? The Tsarevich is still a

33

Nicholas (on the right-hand elephant) in Benares, India, during his travels in the Far East.

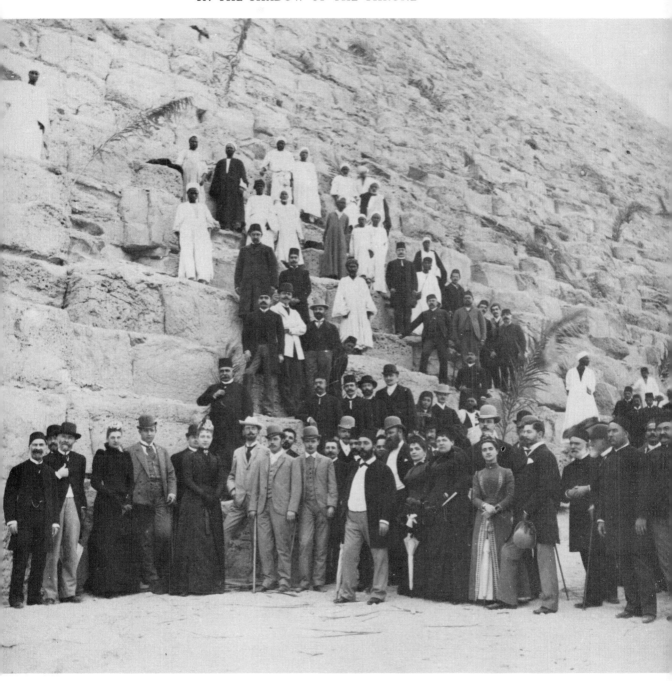

Nicholas and his brother George with friends and attendants in Egypt, 1890.

boy. His opinions are those of a perfect child.' But Witte got his way by arguing that it was important to initiate the heir in affairs of state or he would never understand them.[10]

If Alexander III was troubled by his twenty-four-year-old son's lack of maturity, strangers were struck by the young man's lack of confidence. When Nicholas went to London in 1893 for the wedding of Prince George and Princess May of Teck, he visited the House of Commons. An MP, Mr O'Connor, found the Tsarevich's presence curiously depressing.

The Tsarevich certainly did not give the impression of either mental or physical vigour. It was hard to realize that this slim, not very tall and decidedly delicate looking stripling was the son of the giant who could twist tin plates in the hollow of one of his brawny hands. There was something singular in the manner in which the Tsarevich entered the gallery. . . . He seemed shy, uncertain, indecisive; and altogether went to his place with much awkwardness and shamefacedness. . . .[11]

This was not a happy period in Nicholas's life. Although he continued his affair with Kschessinska, his fondest thoughts were with a beautiful, golden-haired German girl, whose sister Elizabeth was married to his Uncle Serge. Nicholas first met Alix when she was twelve years old and attended 'Ella's' wedding. He was drawn to her even then and gave her a brooch, but she had been taught not to accept presents from 'strangers' and pressed it back into his hand at a children's party.

Alix's credentials were impeccable. Her mother, who had died many years before, was Princess Alice, a daughter of Queen Victoria; and her father, the Grand Duke of Hesse-Darmstadt, was a nephew of the Tsar's mother, another Darmstadt princess. Yet Nicholas did not have an opportunity to see the pretty schoolgirl for another five years. In 1889, when Alix was seventeen, she visited 'Ella' in St Petersburg; and before she left the Tsar gave a party for her at Tsarskoe Selo. The Russian ladies found Alix very beautiful when her countenance was in respose; but the slightest agitation sent a nervous flush across her face that spoiled her appearance. Apart from this, Alix was stiff and unfriendly, and never smiled.

Nicholas was so deeply smitten that he could find no fault in the princess. He was entranced by her lovely face and her wonderful grey-blue eyes. His Uncle Serge guessed his feelings and warned him against 'too much hope' as the Prince of Wales's eldest son, Prince Eddy, had already begun to court Alix. But Nicholas could not stop thinking of her. In 1890, a few weeks before he was to leave on his Far Eastern trip, he learned that Alix was coming to Russia to stay at Serge and Ella's country estate. 'Oh, Lord, how I want to go to Illinskoe,' he wrote in his diary. 'If I do not see her now I shall have to wait a whole year and that would be hard. . . .'

In fact, it was three and a half years before he saw her again. If only he had known the true facts he would have been spared much anguish, for Alix had rejected Eddy's suit almost at once. Of the two men she much preferred the

Alix's parents, the Grand Duke of Hesse-Darmstadt and Princess Alice, with their children. Alix is seated in the left foreground. This photograph was taken about 1878.

*Alix (front row, fourth from the right) during her visit to her
sister Ella. Ella's husband, Nicholas's Uncle Serge,
is the bearded gentleman next to Alix.*

Tsarevich. Queen Victoria did not know the reason for Alix's refusal but
wrote to a friend that her granddaughter had told Eddy that they would not
be happy together and he must not think of her. 'This shows great strength of
character', wrote the Queen, 'as all her family and all of us wish it, and she
refuses the greatest position there is. . . .'

38

In 1892 Prince Eddy died and Nicholas's hopes began to revive. 'My dream is some day to marry Alix of H.,' he wrote in his diary. 'I have loved her a long while and still deeper and stronger since 1889 when she spent six weeks in St Petersburg. For a long time I resisted my feelings, trying to deceive myself by the impossibility, that my dearest wish will come true.' He ended this entry: 'It is all in the hands of God. Relying on his mercy I look forward to the future calmly and obediently.'

The future, however, continued to be hazardous, for that same year the Empress was talking about a possible match between Nicholas and Princess Hélène, the daughter of the Comte de Paris, saying that the alliance might help to strengthen the Russo–Franco Pact, then in the making. 'Two roads seem to be opening before me,' he wrote in his diary. 'I myself want to go in one direction, while it is evident that Mama wants me to chose the other. What will happen?' The question resolved itself as Princess Hélène flatly refused to change her religion; and the forty-nine-year-old Tsar began to suffer from kidney trouble and decided that Nicholas must marry as soon as possible. The doctors came to the conclusion that Alexander III's illness stemmed from injuries contracted five years earlier when the imperial train went off the rails at Borki.

At long last Nicholas had permission to propose to his beloved. The occasion would be the wedding of Alix's brother, now the Grand Duke of Hesse-Darmstadt, to the daughter of the Duke of Edinburgh. Queen Victoria would be much in evidence since both bride and bridegroom were her grandchildren. Indeed the wedding guests represented half the royal houses of Europe – Britain, Germany, Austria, Russia, Denmark, Greece – and included such notable figures as the Prince of Wales and Kaiser Wilhelm II.

Nicholas still faced a formidable hurdle, for Alix was a devout German Lutheran who felt that it would be an affront to God to break her Protestant vows for a new faith bound up with her personal happiness. Nicholas went into battle the day after his arrival but without much success. 'I tried to explain that there was no other way for her than to give her consent,' he wrote to his mother, 'and that she simply could not withhold it. She cried the whole time and only whispered now and then "No, I cannot." Still I went on repeating and insisting ... and although this talk went on for two hours it came to nothing because neither she nor I would give in.'[12]

Everyone at Coburg was so fascinated by the drama that the bride and bridegroom were almost neglected. The relations, wrote Nicky, 'were very touching in their solicitude'; and no one was more touching than the thirty-four-year-old Kaiser. Wilhelm's mother was Queen Victoria's eldest daughter, 'Vicky', a sister of Alix's mother, Alice. Not only was the German Emperor a first cousin, but he knew the Hesse family intimately, for when he was an undergraduate at Bonn University he was a frequent visitor to Darmstadt. He had fallen in love with the fourteen-year-old Elizabeth, now the Grand Duchess Serge, and spent hours writing love poems to her. At that time Alix was only five years old.

Now he was determined to try and persuade her to marry charming Nicky – another cousin, since Nicky's great-grandmother had been a princess of Prussia. To Wilhelm of Hohenzollern the match not only seemed to be made in heaven, but to have a strong earthbound significance as well. Russia and Germany had not been at war since the days of Frederick the Great, and William partially attributed the years of peace to the fact that Russian tsars always married German princesses. There was no reason, he said, for the tradition to end now.

Wilhelm II was in one of his most cheerful and charming moods when he had his talk with Alix. Apparently he brought matters to a successful conclusion for the following day, 8 April, he drove the princess to the house where Nicky was staying and pushed them into a room together. 'We were left alone,' Nicholas wrote to his mother, 'and with her very first words she consented! The Almighty only knows what happened to me then. I cried like a child, and she too; but her expression had changed; her face was lit by a quiet content. ... The whole world is changed for me; nature, mankind, everything; and all seemed to be good and lovable and happy. I couldn't write, my hand trembled so. ...'[13] In his diary he wrote: 'Oh God, what a mountain has rolled from my shoulders. ... The whole day I have been walking in a dream. ... William [the Kaiser] sat in the next room and waited with the uncles and aunts until our talk was over. I went straight with Alix to the Queen [Victoria]. ... The whole family was simply enraptured.'

From then on Nicholas lived in a state of euphoria. He returned to Russia for a few weeks and then he hurried off to join Alix who was staying with her sister Victoria, the wife of Prince Louis of Battenberg. The English trip was idyllic; first, the Battenberg house at Walton-on-Thames, then Windsor Castle with 'Granny'. Years later, Nicholas and Alexandra still delighted in recalling the boat trips, the picnics under the chestnut trees, the walks across beautiful green lawns.

Nicholas discovered that his fiancée was a solemn girl whose life was dominated by a deep religious fervour. Her mother had died when she was six years old; she had recovered from the shock and loneliness through a childish belief in God's love which had grown into a burning faith. Queen Victoria had watched over her daughter's children. They continued to have English nannies and spent several months every year with the Queen at Windsor, Balmoral or Osborne. Yet Alix was not in the least English. She had none of the easy-going ways of her mother's people, and very little sense of humour. She had no use for frivolous individuals and retained a Victorian dislike of 'wasting time' that kept her embroidering and sewing for hours at a time. Her intensity always seemed a little exaggerated and her persistence was thoroughly German. Perhaps her most unfortunate quality was a lack of sensitivity that made her unaware of giving offence.

'Granny' greeted them at Windsor as warmly as though they were her own children. She thought that Nicky was the most civilized Russian she had met, and was delighted that 'Alicky' would be on hand to keep him in order. The

OPPOSITE A triptych belonging to the Tsarina Alexandra.
St Nicholas is flanked by SS Michael and Alexander Nevsky.

ABOVE Alexandra as a young woman.
OPPOSITE Watercolours painted by Nicholas's daughters, the Grand Duchesses.

Tsar had sent his own priest, Father Yanishev, all the way from St Petersburg to Windsor to begin Alix's religious instruction. So while she spent the morning studying, Nicholas galloped through the park and reflected on his immense good fortune. Alix discovered that he was keeping a diary and began to write in it herself: 'I dreamed that I was loved, I woke and found it true and thanked God on my knees for it. True love is the gift which God has given, daily, stronger, deeper, fuller, purer.'

Soon after his arrival Nicholas presented his engagement gifts to his fiancée and Queen Victoria looked on with amazement while her granddaughter examined a necklace of large pink pearls, a pearl ring, a sapphire and diamond brooch, a bracelet with a huge emerald. Most sensational of all was a fabulous cross of pearls, against a blue and white background, created by Fabergé, the famous Russian court jeweller.

During the long journey home, Nicholas often took out his diary to read Alix's parting words: 'I am yours, you are mine, of that be sure. You are locked in my heart, the little key is lost, and now you must stay there forever.' However, when he reached St Petersburg he was forced to put his mind on other things for his mother was alarmed by the Tsar's continued ill health. A doctor summoned from Vienna diagnosed dropsy; although he told the Tsar's brother, the Grand Duke Vladimir, that the end was near, he spared the Empress and recommended the soft air of the Crimea. In October the imperial yacht dropped anchor at Yalta. Alexander had never liked the lovely palace at Livadia, with its orangeries and oleanders, built for his ailing mother, but he was too ill to ignore the doctor's advice. The crowds that gathered at the port were shocked by his appearance. The giant frame was all bones, and the ghostly skin and sunken cheeks wore the look of death.

Nicholas was permitted to ask his fiancée to join him and Alix replied that she would come at once. His relief spilled into his diary: 'My God, what a joy to meet her in my country and to have her near. Half my fears and sadness have disappeared.' He met her train in Simferopol, a four-hour drive away, and brought her to Livadia in an open carriage, accompanied by one of his uncles. Although the Tsar was suffering from headaches and nose bleeds and had such swollen legs that he could scarcely move, he insisted on putting on a full dress uniform and being helped into an armchair where he could greet his son's fiancée with appropriate dignity. Alix knelt by his chair to receive his blessing and asked to be admitted into the Orthodox Church as soon as possible. Within a fortnight the ceremony took place and the twenty-two-year-old German princess emerged as 'the truly believing Alexandra Fedorovna'.

Alexander III lingered for ten days. Five doctors were present; and John of Kronstadt, the famous priest who, many people believed, could perform miracles, spent hours in the sick-room. As court officials and nurses bustled around taking their orders from the Empress, Nicholas and Alexandra were almost forgotten. At first Alix accepted the unusual circumstances, then she began to take umbrage at the neglect, not of herself but of Nicky. Soon he

OPPOSITE Nicholas and his fiancée on the day of their engagement, 8 April 1894.

would be Tsar of all the Russias, yet he was being treated like a nobody. Without a moment's hesitation she threw herself into the breach and began to give advice; and what advice it was! Ignoring the momentous hours all were living through, she urged her fiancé to assert himself and not to allow his distraught mother to take precedence over him.

Don't feel too low [Alexandra wrote in Nicholas's diary]. Your Sunny is praying for you and the beloved patient. . . . Be firm and make the doctors come to you every day and tell you how they find him . . . so that you are always the first to know. Don't let others be put first and you left out. You are Father's dear son and must be told all and asked about everything. Show your own mind and don't let others forget who you are. Forgive me, Lovy.

On 1 November Nicholas's brother-in-law Sandro arrived at Livadia. 'Nicky and I stood on the veranda of the beautiful palace . . . armed with bags of oxygen and watching the end of the Colossus. . . . Alexander died as he had lived, a bitter enemy of resounding phrases, a confirmed hater of melodrama. He just murmured a short prayer and kissed his wife.'[14]

2

Uneasy Lies the Head

'I am not ready to be the Tsar. ... I don't even know how to talk to my ministers,' wept the twenty-six-year-old Emperor Nicholas II to his cousin, the Grand Duke Alexander. Although he had known for many weeks that there was no hope for his forty-nine-year-old father, when death actually came the shock was traumatic. 'Even Alicky could not help him,' his sister, the Grand Duchess Olga, wrote many years later. 'He was in despair. He kept saying that he did not know what would become of us all, that he was wholly unfit to reign. ...'

Nicholas's emotions were in such a turmoil he was unable to exert himself in any direction. 'It was the death of a saint,' he wrote in his diary. 'Oh! God help us during these dreadful days! Poor dear Mama! In the evening at half past nine we had prayers – in the room where he died! I feel as if I were dead myself. ...' Even his reference to his fiancée was depressing for he ended his entry with the words: 'My darling Alix's feet have begun to hurt her.'

Fortunately the Prince of Wales and his wife, Princess Alexandra, a sister of the widowed Empress Marie, arrived at Livadia within forty-eight hours of the Emperor's death. While Alexandra comforted her distraught sister, the Prince injected new courage into demoralized court officials and pacified weeping servants. He even exerted his authority over the dead Tsar's two brothers, Vladimir and Serge, and supervised the arrangements for the body to be taken by cruiser, with suitable escort, to Sebastapol; and from Sebastapol by an imperial train, draped in black, the 1,400 miles across Russia to Moscow and St Petersburg. 'I wonder', mused the Grand Duchess Olga Alexandrovna when she wrote her memoirs, 'what Queen Victoria would have said if she had been present to see everybody accept Uncle Bertie's authority! In Russia of all places!'[1]

The funeral took place in St Petersburg where the Prince of Wales was joined by an equerry, Lord Carrington. The open coffin lay in state for two weeks in the Cathedral of St Peter and St Paul; and the royal mourners had to undergo the ordeal of kissing the dead Emperor's lips. 'As he lay uncovered in his coffin', wrote Carrington, 'his face looked dreadful and the smell was awful. He was not embalmed until three days after his death.'

The Prince of Wales was impressed by the dominance which the Dowager Empress asserted over the young Tsar. Ten days after the funeral, court mourning was suspended for a day so that Nicholas could marry his princess (a niece of Uncle Bertie) who became known in the capital as 'the funeral bride'. Yet his mother refused to allow him to retreat to Tsarskoe Selo after the ceremony, insisting, rather fancifully, that she could not bear to be 'alone'.

OPPOSITE Nicholas and Alix during the early years of their marriage, with Queen Victoria and the Prince of Wales, later Edward VII.

Dutifully he brought his bride back to the Anitchkov Palace and moved into the rooms that he and his brother George had shared as boys. The Prince of Wales, startled by this departure from Victorian decorum, reported to Lord Carrington that the couple came down to breakfast 'as though nothing had happened'.

Not unexpectedly the Prince reached the conclusion that Nicholas II was 'as weak as water'. The new sovereign did not try to conceal his apprehension at the thought of ruling 133,000,000 people, twice the number as in his great-grandfather's day, and talked about his accession as 'an ordeal which I have always dreaded'.

It is not surprising that Nicholas II was daunted, for the Tsar of all the Russias not only wielded absolute power, but found himself in control of a bureaucracy so vast that it comprised a tenth of the nation's urban male population. Throughout the nineteenth century successive tsars had refused to allow foreign banks – or private individuals – to finance Russia's expansion, insisting that all expansion, even economic, was the sole preserve of the government. 'Thus, long before Marxist socialism was so much as dreamed of the Russian State became the largest landowner, the largest factory owners, the largest employer of labour, the largest trader, the largest owner of capital, in Russia, or in the world . . . this brought into being the world's largest apparatus of bureaucracy.'[2]

The hundreds of thousands of officials, ranging from ministers of state and governors to postal workers and policemen, moved up a ladder whose places had been rigidly defined by Peter the Great. Each rank had its appointed uniforms, its privileges, pay and, finally, its pensions. All power resided in the hands of the Tsar and filtered downwards. He had a council of ministers to advise him, who held office at his pleasure, which was notoriously fitful. He could dismiss any one of them at a snap of his fingers. No one, whether governor or church leader or army commander, could wield authority without his personal assent. Even such momentous decisions as war and peace rested with the Tsar alone: and the Tsar was responsible only to God.

Despite Nicholas's forebodings, 1894 was a good year for a beginner, since the country was enjoying a mild industrial boom. It had become a large producer of oil and metals, and was beginning to make its own locomotives and agricultural machinery. Even the peasants, who had suffered a three-year grain famine in 1891–3, were revelling in a bumper harvest. It was an untroubled moment, and Nicholas made a cautious start, his uncles encouraging him to work quietly from home – in this case his suite at the palace. His former schoolroom was transformed into an office, and here he received a steady flow of ministers and officials. 'Petitions and audiences without end,' he grumbled, 'saw Alix for an hour only'; and again, 'I am indescribably happy with Alix. It is sad that my work takes so many hours which I would prefer to spend exclusively with her.'

Although Nicholas wore his love on his sleeve for everyone to see, it was not easy to gauge the depths of Alexandra's feelings. Not until after the

Industrial expansion in late nineteenth-century Russia. The electricity
works in Moscow, on the banks of the Moskva river.

revolution, when imperial diaries and letters were published, did the world
learn how intense was the passion that burned within her, like the deep
hidden fires of a volcano. 'Never', she wrote in her husband's diary, the day
after her wedding, 'did I believe there could be such utter happiness in this
world, such a feeling of unity between two mortal beings. I love you – these
three little words have my life in them.' A week later she wrote even more
ecstatically : 'Never can I thank God enough for the treasure he has given me
for MY VERY OWN – and to be called yours, darling, what happiness can be
greater?'

During the first months of his reign Nicholas was so busy that the days flew
by, but Alexandra had few reserves to fall back on. She never succeeded in
mastering the Russian language as her sister, the Grand Duchess Serge, had
done and therefore had no direct contact with humble people. She spent time
each day in prayer and contemplation, and whatever intellectual curiosity she
possessed was devoted to studying the history of the Orthodox Church and
the miracles performed by the holy men of Russia.

The Empress's greatest fault lay in her inability to hide her feelings. A puritan by nature, she disapproved of the rich, pleasure-loving ladies who surrounded the Dowager Empress. Needless to say, they in turn found the Tsarina intolerably priggish. Behind her back they laughed at her 'German provincialism'. Her unpopularity was inevitable; yet it had the effect of making her more inflexible than ever. Even her initial enthusiasm for 'Motherdear' began to wane. As she sat silently through long dinners at the Dowager Empress's table, she grew to resent the fact that Marie treated the Tsar like a schoolboy, and talked across her daughter-in-law as though she were a nobody. Even more unbearable was Marie's habit of wheedling Nicky into remaining behind after dinner on the pretext of discussing family affairs. Although Alexandra was only twenty-three, with a character not yet clearly defined, her Aunt Vicky, the Dowager Empress of Germany, had written to Queen Victoria that 'Alix is very imperious and will always insist on having her own way; she will never yield one iota of the power she will imagine she wields. . . .'[3]

Alexandra was not yet sure how to exert her authority. Her only friend was her English nanny, Mrs Orchard, who had come from Darmstadt to join her. They sat together sewing for hours at a time. 'I feel myself completely alone,' she wrote in a fit of melancholy to a friend in Germany, Countess Rantsau, 'I weep and I worry all day long because I feel that my husband is so young and so inexperienced ... I am alone most of the time. My husband is all day occupied and he spends his evenings with his mother.'[4] However, her moods changed and a few weeks later she wrote to her sister: 'How contented and happy I am with my beloved Nicky.'

In May 1895, the Dowager Empress went to Denmark for the summer and Nicholas and Alexandra escaped to Peterhof on the Gulf of Finland. In September they moved into the Alexander Palace in Tsarskoe Selo which remained their home for twenty-two years. The village, only fourteen miles from St Petersburg, had sprung into being at the beginning of the eighteenth century when Peter the Great's wife expressed a desire for a country retreat to which she could escape from the granite city her husband was building on the Neva. Since that time a charming tree-lined street had come into being, flanked by houses belonging to courtiers and relations of the royal family.

The imperial park was surrounded by an ornate iron fence and consisted of 800 acres of green lawns studded with flowerbeds and pagodas, lakes, follies and obelisks. Inside were two great palaces designed by two famous Italian architects; the first, constructed by Rastrelli at the command of Catherine the Great, was a huge blue and white structure, very ornate, consisting of 200 rooms. The second was commissioned by Catherine's grandson, Alexander I, and built by Quarenghi after Napoleon's defeat in 1812. It was half the size of Catherine's palace and by comparison strikingly simple – a main building flanked by two wings. The centre contained formal state rooms; one wing provided apartments for the court minister and ladies- and gentlemen-in-waiting; the second wing was the family house of the Tsar and Tsarina.

The Alexander Palace at Tsarskoe Selo.

The palace had been unoccupied for many years. The wing into which Nicholas and Alexandra was moving was dark and ugly, and was re-done at Alexandra's request. Nicholas wrote ecstatically to his mother that although they were sad to leave Peterhof:

When we entered Alix's apartments our mood changed instantly and we could hardly recover from a feeling of pleasant surprise when we saw that nothing had been left even to remind us of the dreadful old arrangement. And this changed to sheer delight when we settled ourselves into these marvellous rooms; sometimes we simply sit in silence wherever we happen to be and admire the walls, the fireplaces, the furniture . . . the mauve room is delightful – one wonders when it looks better, in the evening or by daylight? The bedroom is gay and cosy; Alix's first room, the Chippendale drawing-room, is also attractive, all in pale green; but as not all the furniture is ready yet, it is too early to form a definite opinion about it. In my study and in the dining-room the stoves have been altered and new curtains hung. Twice we went up to the nursery; here also the rooms are remarkably airy, light and cosy.[5]

The nurseries were important – Alexandra was expecting her first baby.

They decided that if it were a boy they would name it Paul. But Mother dear wrote back hastily; '*Paul* for the *first* somehow frightens me a little; still there is time to talk about that. . . . It is understood isn't it, that you will let me know as soon as the first symptoms appear? I shall fly to you, dear children, and shall not be a nuisance, except perhaps by acting as *policeman* to keep everybody else away. . . .'[6]

The baby was born in the middle of November 1895 and named Olga. The disappointment of not having a son was quickly forgotten. 'You can imagine our intense happiness,' the Empress wrote to one of her sisters, 'now that we have such a precious little one to look after and care for.'

Each new tsar brought with him a honeymoon of hope. In the nineties the intelligentsia talked of the growing desire for a free press and a parliamentary government. Some of them predicted that Nicholas II would follow the liberal path of his grandfather, Alexander II, but others, better acquainted with his views, shook their heads. At the time of the funeral, the Prince of Wales had told Lord Carrington that he was disturbed by the young Tsar's slavish adherence to his father's autocratic ideas and his total lack of worldly sense. Carrington replied gloomily that a revolution was inevitable, and the Prince snapped back that nothing was inevitable if Nicky moved with the times. Unfortunately Nicky's only concern was to behave in a way that 'dear saintly Papa' would have approved.

As a result Nicholas's first great official function was a disaster. It took place in the Winter Palace in January 1896, at the end of the period of mourning, and four months before the coronation. Here he received the dignitaries of the Empire, many of them leaders of local governments, or *Zemstvos* as they were called, from all the great cities of Russia. Every group had sent him a written address congratulating him on his accession and commenting on the task that lay before him. The most outspoken observations came from the *Zemstvo* of Tver, famous for its liberal views. This delegation, in muted and respectful language, put forward a mild request 'for the voices of the people to be heard'.

We expect, Gracious Sovereign, that these representative bodies will be allowed to voice their opinion in matters in which they are concerned . . . so that the needs and thoughts . . . of the whole Russian nation might reach the Throne.[6]

If Nicholas had been wise he would have ignored the aspirations behind the soft words from Tver and thanked the delegation for its protestations of loyalty. Instead he delivered a pronouncement that broke on the assembly like a clap of thunder. He rejected the mildest form of representative government as 'a senseless dream' and declared that he would 'maintain for the good of the whole nation the principle of absolute autocracy as firmly and as strongly as did my late father'.

The phrase 'senseless dreams' not only resounded from one end of Russia to the other, but clanged through the revolutionary world as urgently as a fire-bell. First, it sparked off the formation of the Social Revolutionary Party which grew into one of the two major anti-monarchical parties in the country. Second, under the auspices of 'the SRs' a Battle Organization sprang into being in 1902 which let loose a new wave of political assassinations.

The Russian refugees who formed the Executive Revolutionary Committee of Geneva warned Nicholas what to expect. They published an open letter, addressed to the Tsar, which they smuggled into Russia and distributed to every part of the country.

> Your speech has proved that every desire on the part of the nation to be other than slaves kissing the ground before the throne ... is only met with a brutal rebuff. ... The determination to fight to the bitter end against a hateful order of things has been strengthened ... it will not be long before you find yourself entangled in it.[7]

Later, the Procurator of the Holy Synod blamed the Empress for Nicholas's ill-chosen words. 'Our country is prosperous,' he said, 'it is at peace, Nihilism has been destroyed. What earthly reason was there to hurl a threat at the head of the entire nation? But ... she [the Empress] is pursued by the idea that the Emperor does not assert himself sufficiently.'[8]

An especially unhappy event, of a different nature, took place during the coronation festivities in Moscow. According to custom there was always a large fair, enlivened by merry-go-rounds and puppet shows, at which every newly crowned tsar presented gifts to the populace; and on this occasion Khodynka field, on the outskirts of Moscow, was selected for the fête. The choice seems questionable, since the field was normally used as military training ground and was criss-crossed with ditches. Nevertheless the Governor-General of Moscow, the Grand Duke Serge, uncle of the Emperor, brother-in-law of the Empress, approved the plans.

Although a crowd of nearly half a million people was expected from all over Russia, the Grand Duke sent only one squadron of Cossacks and a small detachment of police to maintain order. Early in the morning people began to gather outside the fence that protected the field, watching carts laden with beer, and more carts bearing the eagerly sought gifts – enamel mugs stamped with the double-headed eagle – lumber on to the grounds while helpers arranged the stalls and the theatre booths.

Suddenly, around mid-morning, a rumour swept through the mass that there would not be enough cups to go around, and before anyone knew what was happening a stampede had begun. The field was transformed into a mass of stumbling, screaming, suffocating, kicking humanity. Over 2,000 people were trampled to death.

The imperial party was not due to arrive for several hours, and the head of the police came to an astonishing decision: all signs of the catastrophe would be concealed. 'Peasant carts were requisitioned and the dead bodies carried away in all haste. Finally, when it was realized that it would be quite

Part of the coronation procession, May 1896.

impossible to dispose of the innumerable corpses in time, the floor of the imperial pavilion, from which the Emperor with his guests were to view the festival, was removed and piles of dead men, women and children were thrust under it.'[9] The Grand Duke Alexander, one of the imperial guests, speaks of passing wagons laden with dead bodies. 'The cowardly chief of police', he wrote, 'tried to distract the attention of the Tsar by asking him to acknowledge the cheers of the populace. Each "hurrah" sounded to me like a slap in the face.'[10]

The Tsar and Tsarina were stunned when they were told about the tragedy on their way home. At first Nicholas flatly refused to attend the great ball being given that night by the French Ambassador, the Comte de Montebello. Then the Grand Dukes weighed in and told him that he had no right to offend

56

his 'only European ally'. The French government had spent thousands of pounds sending silver plate and priceless tapestries from Paris and Versailles; it was his duty to make a brief appearance.

It seems incredible that Nicholas and Alexandra could have accepted such bad advice. Nevertheless, they arrived at the Embassy and led the first quadrille. Apparently this was a feat in itself since two hours earlier dozens of police minions had swarmed into the residence saying that a bomb was concealed in one of the flowerpots. They had un-potted over 2,000 plants and, according to a British guest, had transformed the ballroom into a ploughed field.

A garbled account of the imperial couple dancing at the French Embassy, while thousands of people mourned their dead, spread like wildfire and provoked shocked comments. There were a few notable exceptions. Serge Witte wrote that

> Li Hung Chang, who happened to be in St Petersburg on business, was curious to know the details of the catastrophe and I told him that nearly two thousand people must have perished.
> 'But his Majesty', he said, 'does not know it, does he?'
> 'Of course he knows it,' I replied. 'All the facts of the matter must have been reported to him.'
> 'Well,' remarked the Chinaman, 'I don't see the wisdom of that. I remember when I was Governor-General, ten million people died from the bubonic plague in the provinces confined to my charge, yet our Emperor knew nothing about it. Why disturb him uselessly?'[11]

Unfortunately, most people did not see eye to eye with the Chinese plenipotentiary; and the Tsarina never managed to overcome the notoriety of the Khodynka disaster, which marked her official entry into Russian affairs. People branded her as 'cold and heartless' and the words clung throughout Nicholas's reign. 'She . . . did not seem to possess the talent of drawing people to her,' wrote Princess Radziwill, describing the Empress's first court ball. 'She danced badly, not caring for dancing; and she certainly was not a brilliant conversationalist.' Apparently even her beauty went unnoticed, as it was spoiled by a bad complexion. 'She had red arms, red shoulders, and a red face which always gave the impression that she was about to burst into tears. . . . Everything about her was hieratic to the very way she was dressed in the heavy brocade of which she was so fond, and with diamonds scattered all over her, in defiance of good taste and common sense.'[12]

The diamonds represented a minor triumph. Traditionally a widowed empress always sent the State jewels to the reigning empress, but Dowager Empress Marie loved the necklaces and diadems and could not bear to part with them. She resumed her former gay life and soon became a familiar figure in the capital, riding down the Nevsky Prospect in an open carriage pulled by magnificent black trotters, with a huge, bearded Cossack standing on the running board behind her. Alexandra not only resented the jewellery but she was disconcerted to find that the Dowager still took precedence over her.

According to Russian protocol the widow of an emperor always led official processions on the arm of the tsar, while the tsarina followed, accompanied by the senior grand duke.

The circumstances were not conducive to healing the breach, and Alexandra, who had the good sense never to criticize her mother-in-law, told her husband that she no longer wanted the jewels and would not wear them in any case. He passed this message on to his mother, who knew that the Tsarina would be obliged to display them on special occasions and, sensing the breath of a scandal, hastily dispatched them to Alexandra. The Empress marked the event by wearing the gems in great profusion.

If Alexandra disappointed court circles, she in turn viewed the establishment with deep disapproval. 'I feel', she wrote during the first years of her marriage, 'that no one is doing his duty for Russia but only for his own selfish interests. ...' At first the imperial couple spent several months each year in the Winter Palace and Alexandra tried to inject a serious note into the general frivolity. 'Most Russian girls', she complained to her friend Anna Vyrubova, 'seem to have nothing in their heads but officers.'

The Empress, [wrote Anna] coming from a small German Court where everybody tried to occupy themselves usefully, found the idle and listless atmosphere of Russia little to her taste. In her first enthusiasm of power she thought to change things a little for the better. One of her early projects was a society of handiwork composed of ladies of the Court and society circles, each of whom should make with her own hands three garments a year to be given to the poor.[13]

Unfortunately the butterflies were not interested in good works; and Alexandra made no further effort to be convivial. Gradually the imperial balls ended and in their place came theatricals which no one enjoyed. Then the theatricals ceased and the lights went out in the drawing-rooms of the Winter Palace. Nicholas and Alexandra spent most of their time quietly at Tsarskoe Selo, living as much as possible like a private family, forgetting that the nobility – whose ramifications spread across the whole of Russia – was the prop on which the monarchy rested. Alexandra, of course, had an impeccable excuse. During the first six years of her marriage she tried – and failed – to give her husband an heir to the throne, but she produced four daughters: Olga, Tatiana, Marie and Anastasia.

Nicholas did everything he could to model himself on his father, adopting the same political views, even the same prejudices. Like his father he had hardly a drop of Russian blood in his veins, but he dressed in the baggy trousers and blouses of the *moujik* and pursued a relentless policy of Russification. Although he forced the Russian language on to Poles and Finns and Lithuanians, the motivating thrust was religious. 'Russia for the Russians', Witte pointed out sarcastically, 'is for those who belong to the Greek Orthodox Church and whose names end in "ov".'

Nicholas believed that he had been anointed by God and that all peasants everywhere revered him as a Little Father; only the intelligentsia opposed him, and most of them were Jews. He spoke contemptuously of 'Yids' and did nothing to stop the periodic pogroms that swept the country. He admired the army and revelled in the countryside, where his hobbies included cutting wood and building fences.

Last, and most important, Nicholas was perfectly happy to see no one but his wife and children.

During the whole period of my service at Court, [wrote General Mossolov] not a single person was ever invited to go and see Their Majesties after dinner. For their part, Their Majesties never went to see anybody except the Dowager Empress and the Grand Duchess Xenia. . . . The evenings passed very quietly. At first the Empress remained in the drawing room while the Tsar played dominoes or bezique; she would sing a couple of songs. As her health grew worse she came down more and more rarely even for dinner. She dined alone, or with the Tsar, 'alone-together' as the formula ran. . . .[14]

Although, like Alexander III, Nicholas was devoted to his family, in other ways he was not in the least like his father. He was lacking in self-confidence and was so secretive that he even refused to have a secretary, because he regarded all secretaries as spies. Although official documents were drawn up by the ministers concerned, the Tsar took upon himself endless trivialities, such as filing correspondence, noting reports and assembling ideas for speeches. 'He was so jealous of his prerogatives', wrote the head of the court chancellery, 'that he himself sealed the envelopes containing his decisions. He had to be very busy before he could entrust his valet with this trivial task. And the valet had to show the sealed envelopes, so that his master could satisfy himself that the secrecy of his correspondence was inviolate.'[14]

Even more unlike his father, Nicholas could never bring himself to speak openly and honestly to the officials who served him.

The Tsar's contribution to a talk, [wrote General Mossolov] was never sharp or direct, never argumentative. . . . The Minister would take his leave, delighted at having, to all appearances, carried his point. But he would be sadly mistaken. What he had taken for weakness was merely dissimulation. He had forgotten that the Tsar was absolutely without moral courage; that he loathed making a final decision in the presence of the person concerned. Next day the Minister would receive a letter from him – a letter of dismissal. . . . Nicholas II . . . had an unmistakable faith in the providential nature of his high office. His mission emanated from God. For his actions he was responsible only to his own conscience and to God. . . . Responsible to imponderables; to the mysticism that steadily increased its hold over him.[14]

Was the Tsar weak? Or was he treacherous? Perhaps Wilhelm of Germany found the answer when he said: 'The Tsar is not treacherous but he is weak. Weakness is not treachery, but it fulfils all its functions.'[15] Occasionally the treachery was premeditated. In 1896–7 Nicholas almost plunged Russia into war in order to seize the Turkish Straits which had always been his father's dearest wish. Nicholas had no clear-cut plan, and his mind swung like a

Nicholas (OPPOSITE with Olga, born in 1896) was a devoted family man. ABOVE His second daughter Tatiana, born in 1897 (LEFT), and (RIGHT) his third daughter Marie, born in 1899.

pendulum between one impulse and the next.

Nicholas had extravagant ambitions and liked to imagine the Ship of State setting forth on a voyage of high adventure. 'I told Witte', wrote General Kuraptkin in 1896, 'that our Tsar had grandiose plans in his head: to capture Manchuria for Russia and to annex Korea. He is dreaming also of bringing Tibet under his dominion. He desires to take Persia, and to seize not only the Bosphorus, but the Dardanelles.'[16]

The question of the Bosphorus arose when the Russian Ambassador to Constantinople, Nelidov, presented Nicholas with an incredibly harebrained scheme which the latter seized upon with boyish enthusiasm. The Turks once again had outraged European feeling by carrying out a massacre – this time against the Armenians – and the ambassador insisted that the time was ripe for Russia to 'create incidents' in Constantinople; and with no warning, no declaration of war, to dispatch flotillas from Odessa and Sebastopol with 30,000 troops aboard who would land on both sides of the Straits and seize the heights above Constantinople. His proposal envisaged a bold *coup de main*, a sort of lightning commando raid which would be an accomplished fact before Britain or any other great power realized what was happening.

Although this scheme was both foolish and impractical, Nicholas II was delighted with it. Just as his father had encouraged underhand moves against fellow monarchs, Nicholas warmed to the suggestion of plotting against 'the most unorthodox and unbelieving Sultan'. He particularly relished the idea of Nelidov creating 'incidents', and approved the cloak-and-dagger signal of readiness in the form of a telegram to Russia's financial agent in London concerning the purchase of grain.

Serge Witte, the Minister of Finance, fought the plan vehemently and insisted that his own opposition be put in writing; when Nicholas refused

Railway-building was the key to Russian expansion in the East.

62

to be deterred Witte approached both the Dowager Empress and Pobedonostsvev. The latter held up his hands and exclaimed: '*Jacta est alea. God help Russia!*' Perhaps one or other of these persons interfered, for Nicholas finally accepted the possibility that Britain and Austria might make war on behalf of Turkey, and cancelled the project.

The Tsar's impulses were erratic. Two years later he had put the idea of force out of his mind and proposed a peace conference to be held at The Hague, at which the limitation of arms would be discussed. Apparently Russia was engaged in re-organizing her infantry and could not afford the increases in artillery being planned in Austria–Hungary. Twenty European powers accepted the invitation, since none wished to be branded as warmongers, but privately they criticized the conference and agreed with the Prince of Wales when he described it as 'the greatest nonsense and rubbish I ever heard of'. Unfortunately, the Hague conception soon gave way to a third impulse which ended in a disastrous war for Russia.

Nicholas II's ill-fated adventure in the Far East began in 1896 when China accorded Russia the right to extend the Trans-Siberian Railway across the north of Manchuria, and later granted her a ninety-nine year lease of Port Arthur. 'Glad news . . . ,' Nicholas had written. 'At last we shall have an ice-free port.' Several years later the Boxer Rebellion of 1900 gave the Tsar a pretext for occupying the whole of Manchuria, which he did against the advice of his ministers who foresaw trouble with the Japanese. If Nicholas had recognized Korea as a province essential to Japan's security he could have reached an agreement with the Mikado; but he had designs on Korea himself, and refused to negotiate.

During this period the youthful, exuberant Emperor of Germany, Wilhelm II, gave Nicholas great encouragement. Wilhelm was anxious to divert Russia from the Balkans where she was likely to clash with Germany's ally, Austria–Hungary. 'We must try to tie Russia down to East Asia,' he confided to one of his ministers, 'so that she pays less attention to Europe and the Near East.' To Nicholas he talked endlessly about 'the Yellow Peril' and Russia's duty to defend Europe against 'the Mongols and the Buddhists'.

Nicholas was enthusiastic about the idea of a Far Eastern venture, particularly if he could achieve his aims without much cost. He therefore listened to the suggestions of a group of Russian adventurers led by a retired cavalry captain, Bezobrazov. This gentleman was eager to get a large grant of money from the Treasury in order to finance a private company in Korea to exploit the Korean forests. Russia, he said, could move her soldiers into the territory disguised as workmen and perhaps seize control of the area unnoticed.

Once again the Tsar was attracted by a scheme that was both treacherous and puerile. Witte said the money was not available and protested vehemently that 'an armed struggle with Japan . . . would be a great disaster'; even if Russia won, the conflict would be bound to stimulate

Count Witte was relieved of his post as Minister of Finance when he tried to dissuade Nicholas from undertaking his harebrained and dangerous schemes in the Far East.

revolutionary activity or, as he put it, to stir up 'the latent dissatisfaction of our domestic life'.[17]

The Tsar insisted on financing Bezobrazov, who set up the Yalu Timber Company in the Yalu River basin. No one regarded it as a private venture. Not only did Bezobrazov boast to everyone that he had the Emperor's support, but the Emperor himself, in the middle of 1903, appointed Admiral Alexeiev to a pretentious new post, Viceroy of the Far East. About the same time, Nicholas relieved Witte of his important position as Minister of Finance and gave him the unimportant post of President of the Committee of Ministers.

This move was noted by the Japanese, who quite rightly interpreted it to mean that Nicholas II was not to be deterred in his ambitions. The Japanese Ambassador in St Petersburg tried in vain to see the Tsar; and finally sent urgent messages warning him that Russia's policy was leading straight to war. But the Tsar refused to take him seriously. The Russians could annihilate the 'Japanese monkeys' merely by throwing their caps in the air. On New Year's day, 1904, the Tsar talked grandly of Russia's military strength and expressed the hope that there would not be a test of his patience.

A month later, in early February, Japanese destroyers made a sudden attack on the Russian squadron in Port Arthur and torpedoed two battleships and a cruiser. 'This without a declaration of war,' declared an outraged Nicholas. 'May God come to our aid.' God appeared reluctant to move, for a month later, when Admiral Makarov sortied from the harbour, his flagship hit a mine and sank with 700 men aboard.

With the sea secured, Japan was able to send her expeditionary force to the mainland, at any point she chose. One army landed in Korea, overwhelmed five Siberian regiments and, after crossing the Yalu River, advanced into northern Manchuria. A second contingent landed at the head of the Yellow Sea, enabling Japanese shock troops to storm the heights around Port Arthur, while giant guns bombarded the harbour. The war news reaching St Petersburg was consistently gloomy and the home front was in a state of permanent disorganization. 'This country has no real government,' lamented the British Chargé d'Affaires.

Each minister acts on his own [he continued] doing as much damage as possible to the other ministers. . . . It is a curious state of things. There is an Emperor, a religious madman almost – without a statesman, or even a council – surrounded by a legion of Grand Dukes – thirty-five of them and not one of them at war at this moment, with a few priests and priestly women behind him. No middle class . . . an underpaid bureaucracy living, of necessity, on corruption. Beneath this, about 100 million of people gradually becoming poorer and poorer as they bear all the burden of taxation, drafted into the army in thousands. . . .[18]

ABOVE Marauding Cossacks in a Korean village.

In January 1905 Port Arthur surrendered, and soon after Mukden fell to the enemy. Although it looked as though defeat were inevitable, Nicholas seized a last chance – regarded by most people as a forlorn hope – to stave off ignominy. He dispatched the Russian Baltic Fleet, under the command of Admiral Rozhdestvensky, in the vain hope of re-establishing Russian naval supremacy.

The Kaiser's merchant ships refuelled the Russian fleet in the French island of Madagascar and the French port of Camranh Bay in Indo-China. But when the eight Russian battleships, steaming in columns, appeared in the Straits of Tsushima, between Korea and Japan, a barrage of Japanese shells blazed into them. The Japanese action commanded by Admiral Togo lasted only forty-five minutes. All eight Russian battleships were sunk, along with seven out of the twelve Russian cruisers and six out of nine destroyers. 'Definite confirmation', Nicholas wrote in his diary, 'of the terrible news concerning the almost complete destruction of our fleet.'

President Theodore Roosevelt of the United States offered to act as an intermediary in securing peace. Without more ado the Tsar summoned Witte and asked him to negotiate. 'When a sewer has to be cleaned, they send for Witte,' the statesman grumbled, but he accepted all the same, and soon was on his way to Portsmouth, New Hampshire, where the conference was scheduled to take place.

Russia's unhappy war in the Far East accelerated the revolutionary movement at home, just as Witte had prophesied. Even before hostilities

Plekhanov, founder of the first Marxist group in Russia.

OPPOSITE One of the magnificent bejewelled Easter eggs made for the imperial family by the court jeweller Fabergé.

began, the terrorists were springing into life again. In 1902 they assassinated Sipyagin, the Minister of the Interior; and in his place the Tsar appointed Vyacheslav Plehve, a tight-lipped reactionary law officer who had won prominence in 1881 for rounding up the killers of Alexander II.

Plehve took his duties as head of the police seriously, and introduced several extraordinary schemes which sometimes brought the opposite result to what he hoped. At that time there were two main revolutionary parties: Social Democrats, 'SDS', who embraced Marxism and concentrated their propaganda on factory workers in urban centres, and Social Revolutionaries, 'SRS', who advocated a socialist society based on the village commune, and worked to provoke an uprising among the peasants. Neither party had more than a few thousand active members and most of their leaders lived in exile abroad.

The creator of the SDS, or Marxist group, was George Plekhanov, the son of a prosperous country gentleman in the Tambov province. Plekhanov should have had a career in the army but at St Petersburg University he became a revolutionary instead. He moved to Geneva to escape the police net, and in 1883, when he was only twenty-six, founded the Liberation of Labour, the first Marxist group in Russian history. One of his faithful followers was the notorious Vera Zasulich who had tried to kill the Chief of the St Petersburg Police by firing two bullets into him, but was later acquitted by a jury.

In 1900 Vladimir Ulyanov, a thirty-year-old lawyer with slanting eyes, a stumpy body and a head like a pumpkin, arrived from Russia to join them.

OPPOSITE Fabergé egg containing miniatures of the imperial palaces, presented to Alexandra by Nicholas in 1896.

Lenin, leader of the breakaway group known as the Bolsheviks.

Later known as Lenin, this man was the son of a mathematics teacher and a well-to-do German woman whose father was a doctor and a landowner. They lived in Simbirsk, a town on the Volga; oddly enough Lenin's headmaster was Fedor Kerensky, the father of Alexander Kerensky who headed the Provisional Government after the revolution. Lenin was successful as a schoolboy. 'Very gifted, always neat and assiduous,' pronounced Fedor. 'Ulyanov was first in all subjects and upon completing his studies won a gold medal.'[19]

Since Lenin's brother, Alexander Ulyanov, had been hanged because of complicity in a plot to murder Nicholas's father, Alexander III, Lenin remained under constant police supervision. Nevertheless, when he went to St Petersburg to study law, he joined a Marxist group. Soon after, as might have been expected, he was arrested for being in possession of illegal literature, and thrown into prison where he spent a year. After that he was sent to Siberia for another three years. But his exile was not disagreeable; in his small village he was able to set up his own household, he had plenty of books, and he even acquired a wife – a serious young woman revolutionary, Nadezhda Krupskaya, under sentence like himself.

When he was free he joined Plekhanov in Geneva, and took on the job of co-editor of *Iskra* (The Flame), a paper that would be smuggled into Russia regularly to promote the Marxist cause. The first issue, which came out in December 1900, was seized by the frontier police and never reached its destination. After that, the underground workers grew more professional. Merchant seamen bound for St Petersburg, and sometimes those *en route* for ports in the Black Sea, were persuaded to deliver the forbidden fruit to its distributors. Once someone tried wrapping the copies in waterproof sheets and dumping them overboard at prearranged points, but apparently too many bundles were lost to make this a permanent arrangement. It was as co-editor that Ulyanov first used the name 'Lenin', writing leaders and articles for every issue and frequently using the royal third person: 'Lenin pointed out. ...' While Plekhanov lived in Geneva, Lenin moved to Munich where the paper was printed. Here he not only established himself as editor-in-chief, but managed to strengthen his control of the underground organization in Russia. By 1903, however, too many disagreements had arisen between the two men, and Plekhanov called a conference in Brussels. Lenin was determined to become master of the party, and the quarrels that broke out were so violent that the Belgian police ordered the delegates to leave the country within twenty-four hours. At this the whole assembly departed for London, where the meeting was resumed.

Lenin believed that his best chance of winning power was to split the party in two, so that he at least could lead one of the factions. He worked like a tornado, lobbying tirelessly, barring all pacifiers from committee meetings and trying instead to inflame and divide opinion. Over one issue, when he saw that he had a majority of two, he called for a vote. He immediately proclaimed that he and his followers were in the majority – Bolsheviks – and his opponents in the minority – Mensheviks. Before the Congress broke up he managed to set up a new editorial board for *Iskra*, consisting only of himself, Plekhanov and a well-known revolutionary, Martov.

What happened next was unexpected. Such a fierce revulsion arose against Lenin that his following began to dwindle and his money funds to freeze. Worst of all, he was forced to resign from the board of *Iskra* because Martov flatly refused to serve with him. Lenin decided to fight another day. He gave up all his party offices and went walking with Nadezhda Krupskaya in Switzerland. His thoughts were so absorbed by his battle with the Mensheviks that he scarcely noticed the outbreak of the Russo–Japanese War.

Meanwhile, the second big revolutionary party – the SRs – were so busy murdering people they had no time to quarrel. In 1902, they set up a Battle Organization pledged to carry on the work of Will of the People, the group that had assassinated Alexander II. At this point the new Minister of the Interior, Vyacheslav Plehve, a man brimming over with new ideas, stepped in. As head of the secret police – the *Okhrana* – he introduced the short-sighted policy of honeycombing the underground parties with *agents provocateurs*. He did not seem to understand that these 'double agents' were obliged to perform valuable services for both sides in order to stay alive.

His most celebrated hireling was Ievno Asev, the son of a poor Jewish family, who had joined the police when he was a student at the Polytechnic in Karlsruhe, studying for a degree in engineering. Asev tried to make friends with the student revolutionaries, but his appearance was so repellent that his overtures were rejected. Everything was wrong with his face. His forehead was low, his lips thick, his ears protruding, his nose flat, his eyes bulging and shifty. Soon he began to run out of money and one day he picked up his pen and wrote to the secret police, giving them details of the revolutionary organizations in the town. He offered to supply information regularly for a fee of fifty roubles a month. The police investigated his background and enrolled him as an agent.

Asev joined the Battle Organization of the Social Revolutionary Party in 1901, and was such an inspired worker that at the end of two years he was offered the leadership. Plehve was delighted. He knew himself to be one of the most feared and hated men in Russia, and almost every terrorist in the country had contemplated killing him at one time or another. With Asev operating as chief of the Battle Organization, Plehve would be not only forewarned, but protected.

At first things worked out as Plehve expected. On several occasions Asev informed the *Okhrana* of plots to murder the Minister, which resulted in arrests. He also put the police on the trail of secret printing presses, explosive arsenals and propaganda depots. He gave them the names of provincial revolutionary societies and, on his travels to Berlin and Paris, kept them informed about emigré conspiracies. But Asev only told the police what he wanted them to know. At the end of his first year as chief of the Battle

Organization the morale of his fellow revolutionaries was so low from repeated failure that Asev decided the time had come to make an impression; since he was a man with a flair for drama, he decided to murder Plehve. No doubt Asev was influenced by Plehve's pogroms against the Jews. Furthermore, Plehve had become careless. Recently an acquaintance had found him walking alone on Aptekarsky Island. He asked the Minister how he ventured to run such a risk when everyone knew that the terrorists were plotting against him. 'Oh, I shall know about all of these plans in good time,' he smiled.

Plehve's murder took place in July 1904. A smart brougham drawn by two horses, its curtains tightly drawn, moved briskly along a tree-lined avenue in St Petersburg conveying the Minister to his weekly meeting with the Tsar. The Minister's carriage passed a vehicle in which was riding Dr E. J. Dillon, the correspondent of the London *Daily Telegraph*, a scholar of international repute. He reported:

Suddenly, the ground before me quivered, a tremendous sound as of thunder deafened me, the windows of the houses on both sides of the broad street rattled, and the glass of the panes was hurled on to the stone pavement. A dead horse, a pool of blood, fragments of a carriage and a hole in the ground were part of my rapid impressions. My driver was on his knees devoutly praying and saying that the end of the world had come. I got down from my seat and moved towards the hole, but a police officer ordered me back, and to my question replied that the Minister, Plehve, had been blown to fragments. . . . [20]

The assassination was front page news all over the world; but how much greater the sensation would have been if the public had known that the murderer was one of the dead Minister's trusted, hand-picked police operators! News of Plehve's death reached Geneva the same day that it happened. On the borders of the lake a group of Social Revolutionaries living in exile were holding a Congress. 'For several minutes', an eye-witness wrote, 'pandemonium reigned. Several men and women became hysterical. Most of those present embraced each other. On every side there were shouts of joy. . . .' Asev had not only re-established his position, but had become the hero of the party.

What explanation did he give to the police? He upbraided them for not having paid more attention to his early warnings, insisting that this last attempt had been made impulsively without his knowledge. Did the *Okhrana* accept the story? Dr Dillon, the Englishman who witnessed the murder, suggested that both the police and government officials suspected Asev's complicity, but that Plehve was so unpopular no one regretted his loss; since the *Okhrana* did not press for an investigation this cynical interpretation could be correct.

In January 1905 the struggle with Japan took a nasty turn. The collapse of Port Arthur was particularly demoralizing since before the war Russian

Nicholas's ambitions in the Far East ended disastrously with ignominious defeat in the Russo–Japanese War. A Japanese caricature of the Tsar playing at soldiers.

generals had boasted about trouncing Japan with a flick of the finger; now it was obvious that they were not even going to win the war. Indeed, faith in the tsardom was dealt such a severe blow that a small strike at the Putilov works in St Petersburg suddenly mushroomed into a mammoth stoppage with thousands of men pouring on to the streets. It was the opening shot of the Russian revolution, still twelve years in the offing.

At this point Father Gapon decided to intervene. This young, thirty-two-year-old priest was one of the recruits of the recently assassinated Minister of the Interior, Plehve. Gapon had been enrolled by the *Okhrana* to promote a crazy concept known as 'police socialism'. The idea was to organize trade unions whose leaders would preach that the Tsar was not responsible for their miseries – the blame belonged to the capitalists who owned the factories! This ridiculous concept appealed to Gapon who formed a huge union called the 'Assembly of the Russian Working Men'. He was an idealist who believed passionately in the peasant–worker myth 'that the Little Father would help them if only the Little Father knew'.

In the atmosphere of disenchantment that existed in the early days of 1905, it was impossible to restore morale, so that Gapon decided to put police socialism – in which he genuinely believed – to the test. He made whirlwind speeches throughout the working-class districts, announcing that on Sunday he would lead a mass march to the Winter Palace and with his own hands give the Tsar a petition stating the grievances and aspirations of the working class.

According to Count Kokovtsov, the Minister of Finance, scarcely one of the Tsar's ministers had ever heard of Father Gapon until the night before the march; even then they knew nothing of his connection with the police. It seems incredible that the new Minister of the Interior, Prince Sviatopolk-Mirsky, should have been so badly informed on Gapon's activities, but it must be remembered that Nicholas II had no Prime Minister, and that the Tsar's advisers never met to discuss important affairs among themselves. All

Count Kokovtsov.

issues were taken straight to the Tsar for his pronouncements alone, and many matters were not regarded as 'issues'.

On the eve of the march, Sviatopolk-Mirsky conferred with the Chief of Staff of the Guards and the Governor-General of St Petersburg and gave orders that the workers were not to be allowed to reach the Winter Palace. 'Troops have been brought from the outskirts to reinforce the garrison,' wrote Nicholas in his study at Tsarskoe Selo. 'Up to now the workers have been calm. Their number is estimated at 120,000. At the head of their union is a kind of socialist priest named Gapon. Mirsky came this evening to present his report on the measures taken.'[21]

One can only marvel at the Tsar's detachment and Mirsky's failure to understand the political importance of the occasion. Nicholas had very little imagination; but Mirsky's attitude is puzzling, and one can only come to the conclusion that it was caused by an unpleasant happening two days earlier. Nicholas was taking part in the traditional ceremony of blessing the waters of the Neva when one of the ceremonial cannons fired a live shell which exploded near the Emperor, wounding a policeman. Although the authorities insisted that the mishap was a *bona fide* accident, no one could be sure.

On Sunday morning Gapon led 200,000 workers towards the palace. Many were carrying banners and ikons and portraits of the Tsar. They locked arms and sang hymns as they flowed along the icy, windswept streets. At various bridges and intersections the marchers suddenly found their way blocked by infantry backed by Cossacks and Hussars. There was not one, mammoth clash, but half a dozen minor confrontations. As the crowd surged forward troops fired point blank into the oncoming mass. The hard-packed snow was stained with blood and littered with banners and ikons as the procession fell back, stumbling, crying, shouting and shaking their fists.

Father Gapon immediately joined the Social Revolutionary Party, proclaiming to the people: 'We no longer have a Tsar. . . . Take bombs and dynamite. I absolve you!' He fled to Switzerland where the revolutionary exiles feted him as a hero; and he issued a statement which rang around the world: 'I call upon all the socialist parties of Russia to come to an immediate agreement among themselves and begin an armed uprising against Tsarism.'

Gapon's march went down into history as 'Bloody Sunday' and historians now interpret this as marking the beginning of the Russian Revolution. Abroad, people were horrified by reports of the shooting. Ramsay Macdonald, a future Labour Prime Minister of Britain, attacked the Tsar as 'a blood-stained creature'; and this impression was so ineradicable that when the revolution came thirteen years later, the British left wing was strongly opposed to giving the imperial family asylum in Britain.

Nicholas declared in his diary that the troops had been forced to fire and there were 'many killed and wounded. Lord, how painful and sad this is!' Alexandra wrote to her sister, Princess Victoria of Battenberg, lamenting her husband's anxieties.

My poor Nicky's cross is a heavy one to bear, all the more as he has nobody on whom he can thoroughly rely and who can be a real help to him. He has had so many bitter disappointments, but through it all he remains brave and full of faith in God's mercy. He tries so hard, works with such perseverance, but the lack of what I call 'real' men is great. . . .

Don't believe all the horrors the foreign papers say. They make one's hair stand on end – foul exaggeration. Yes, the troops, alas, were obliged to fire. Repeatedly the crowd was told to retreat and that Nicky was not in town (as we are living here this winter) and that one would be forced to shoot, but they would not heed and so blood was shed. . . . It is a ghastly thing, but if one had not done it the crowd would have grown colossal and 1000 would have been crushed. All over the country, of course, it is spreading. . . .

Petersburg is a rotten town, not one atom Russian. The Russian people are deeply and truly devoted to their Sovereign and the revolutionaries use his name for provoking them against landlords, etc but I don't know how. . . . Poor Nicky, he has a bitter, hard life to lead. . . .[22]

Stupidly, the government ordered the leading workmen who had taken part in the march to leave the capital. The result was that eye-witness accounts of Bloody Sunday spread across Russia, resulting in a nationwide epidemic of strikes. These stoppages were accompanied by the murder of police officials on an enormous scale. The killings always took place at twilight, and the assassins usually escaped.

Asev added to the reign of terror by ignoring his paymaster, the *Okhrana*, and serving the revolutionaries. Once again he thrilled his fellow conspirators by the boldness of his aims. This time the prospective victim was an uncle of the Emperor and a brother-in-law of the Empress; none other than the Grand Duke Serge, who had just resigned as Governor-General of Moscow, but was still in charge of the city's troops. Asev's target was impeccable, for Serge was bitterly hated by the intelligentsia for his cruelly reactionary views. 'Try as I will,' his cousin wrote, 'I cannot find a single redeeming feature in his character.'

As the Grand Duke left his apartment in the Kremlin and drove through one of the gates, a bomb exploded on top of him. Hearing the terrible blast, Ella, his wife, cried: 'It's Serge!' and ran out to him. All that was left were a hundred fragmented pieces of flesh lying on the hard-packed snow. Later she visited the murderer, a man named Kalayev, in prison. She offered to plead for his life if he would express his sorrow; but Kalayev refused, saying that he could think of no greater happiness than to die for his precious cause.

Ella built a convent of Mary and Martha in Moscow, and became its first abbess. Here she lived and worked. She never wore jewellery again, and always dressed in a long, hooded, pearl-grey robe and a white veil.

Bloody Sunday and the assassination of the Tsar's Uncle Serge took place during the worst phase of the war with Japan. As depressing reports of Russian defeats on sea and land rolled across the empire, violence increased and spread to every town. 'It makes me sick to read the news,' Nicholas wrote

The Tsarina's sister Ella (the Grand Duchess Elizabeth), wife of Grand Duke Serge who was assassinated in 1905.

to his mother. 'Strikes in schools and factories, murdered policemen, Cossacks, riots.' Even then, poor Nicholas was too weak to take control, clinging with tenacious stupidity to the autocracy that he did not know how to use, and blaming others for his misfortunes. 'But the ministers, instead of acting with quick decisions, only assemble in council like a lot of frightened hens and cackle about providing united ministerial action.'[23]

When news came that the Japanese had sunk almost all the ships of the Russian Baltic Fleet at Tsushima, a wave of mutiny swept the navy. Sailors of the battleship *Potemkin* claimed that they were served bad meat and used the excuse to throw their officers overboard. Then they raised the red flag and went steaming along the coast of the Black Sea, mindlessly bombarding towns until lack of fuel forced them to give themselves up in the Romanian port of Constanza.

While Witte was in America that August negotiating the peace with Japan, mutinous soldiers were returning from the east and spreading discontent to the cities. In Moscow a dispute arose among the printers as to whether the men on piece-work should be paid for punctuation marks. This resulted in a 'comma strike' that flared across Russia like some strange, pre-arranged signal. It triggered off a chain of sympathy strikes ranging from railway stoppages to a walk-off by the imperial *corps de ballet*.

The Russian battleship Tsarevich *was one of many ships damaged or destroyed at Tsushima.*

Although the strike had begun in Moscow, it reached its zenith in St Petersburg. Here, almost the whole adult population stopped work. There were no trains, no newspapers, no trams, no post or telegraph, not even any bakers willing to bake bread. As the general strike spread, even Lenin stopped thinking of ways to crush Plekhanov, and went to the Geneva Library to study the art of street fighting. 'I see with real horror', he wrote to his followers in Russia, 'that we have been talking bombs for more than half a year and not one single one has been made.'[24] He recommended 'breaking into banks to raise funds' and sent pages of advice on everything from brass knuckles to dynamite cartridges.

The only revolutionary exile who played a great part *inside* Russia was Lev Bronstein, now known to his comrades as Leon Trotsky. Only twenty-six years old, the son of a Jewish peasant-farmer from the steppes, Trotsky had spent most of his adult life in the grip of the police; two and a half years in Russian prisons and another two years in eastern Siberia. In 1903, he had escaped to Russia and joined Plekhanov and the Mensheviks. But now, in the summer of 1905, the excitement was too much for him and he risked his freedom to return to St Petersburg.

Trotsky was a spell-binding orator and a brilliant organizer, and within a week of his arrival in the capital he had set up a Central Council or 'Soviet' as it was called. The membership consisted of factory workers who had been elected to represent 500 comrades each. The Soviet played the role of an army GHQ, distributing arms and issuing orders in the form of printed bulletins. The orders were ruthless but relevant. The Soviets threatened to wreck any factory that tried to defy the strike and stay open.

By the time Witte returned to Russia in September the whole country lay in the grip of a general strike. In St Petersburg sentries stood nervously guarding the public buildings while squadrons of Cossacks clattered along the empty streets, whips and sabres at hand. Nicholas received Witte on board his yacht. The statesman had to travel to Peterhof by canal boat and carriage since no trains were running. He had done brilliantly well in America, securing far better terms from the Japanese than anyone had felt possible, and Nicholas referred warmly to him in a letter to his mother. 'Witte came to see us,' he wrote, 'he was very charming and interesting. After a long talk I told him of his new honour. I am creating him a count. He went quite stiff with emotion and tried three times to kiss my hand.'[25]

Later, in more letters to his mother, he described the weeks that followed.

So the ominous days began. Complete order in the streets but at the same time everybody knew that something was going to happen. The troops were waiting for a signal, but the other side would not begin. One had the same feeling as before a thunderstorm in summer. Everybody was on edge and extremely nervous. ... Through all those horrible days I constantly met with Witte. We very often met in the early morning to part only in the evening when night fell. There were only two ways open: to find an energetic soldier to crush the rebellion by sheer force. There would be time to breathe then, but likely as not one would have to use force again in a few months, and that would mean rivers of blood and in the end we should be where we started.

The other way would be to give the people their civil rights, freedom of speech and Press, also to have all the laws confirmed by a state Duma – that of course would be a constitution. Witte defends this energetically. . . .[26]

While the Tsar was trying to decide between these alternatives his cousin, the six-foot-six Grand Duke Nicholas, got wind that 'the soldier' they were thinking of to head the dictatorship was none other than himself. He arrived at the palace in Tsarskoe Selo in a state of violent agitation. According to the Head of Chancellery, General Mossolov, the Grand Duke pulled out his revolver and began shouting: 'If the Emperor does not accept the Witte programme, if he wants to force me to become Dictator, I shall kill myself in his presence with this revolver. We must support Witte at all costs. It is necessary for the good of Russia.'[27]

In the end, this was what the Tsar did. Witte assured the sovereign that a constitution was the only way out. Nicholas wrote to his mother:

Almost everybody I had an opportunity of consulting is of the same opinion. Witte put it to me quite clearly that he would accept the Presidency of the Council of Ministers only on condition that his programme was not interfered with. He . . . drew up the Manifesto. We discussed it for two days and in the end, invoking God's help, I signed it. . . . My only consolation is that such is the will of God and this grave decision will lead my dear Russia out of the intolerable chaos she has been in for nearly a year.[26]

The Grand Duke Nicholas Nicolaevich, the Tsar's cousin, was nominated as 'dictator' of Russia in 1905.

The Imperial Manifesto of October 1905 guaranteed freedom of conscience, speech, association and assembly, and promised an elected parliament, or Duma, whose consent would be necessary for any law. Although the Tsar retained immense power by his right to appoint ministers and his prerogative over defence and foreign affairs, he went through weeks of agonizing soul searching before he could bring himself to sign the hated document. He made the move solely because the anarchy continued to grow and Count Witte insisted that the only way to restore order was by issuing the manifesto.

Russia did not quieten down as quickly as Witte hoped. Anarchy had become a way of life and peasants continued to rise against their landlords; savage naval mutinies took place on the Black Sea and the Baltic; and in Poland, Finland and Georgia mass demonstrations demanded autonomy. In December, 2,000 workers organized by the Social Democrats set up a 'provisional government' in Moscow, which was only dispersed when the Semyonovsky Guards were ordered on the scene. Lenin slipped into Russia for a few days, but slipped out again with alacrity when the police got on to his trail.

The Duma in session.

During these weeks of continued violence, Nicholas began to turn against Witte. 'It is strange', he wrote to his mother, 'that such a clever man should be wrong in his forecasts of an easy pacification.' And two weeks later: 'Everyone is afraid of taking courageous action. I keep trying to force them – even Witte himself – to behave more energetically.' But when the Guards Brigades were called to restore order in Moscow, Nicholas was just as critical. 'As for Witte, since the happenings in Moscow he has radically changed his views, now he wants to hang and shoot everybody. I have never seen such a chameleon of a man. That, naturally, is why no one believes in him any more.'[28]

Count Witte was aware of the Tsar's coldness and tried to reinstate himself by a number of arbitrary additions to the 'Fundamental Laws' which gave the Duma its constitutional rights. The Emperor snatched back total control of the army and navy and also established the right to pass any law he liked when the Duma was not sitting. Despite these revisions, Nicholas II asked for Witte's resignation on the eve of the parliamentary opening, appointing in his place an aged and incompetent reactionary, Ivan Goremykin.

The Tsar gave a reception for the newly elected deputies in the throne room of the Winter Palace. Since the revolutionaries boycotted the election, the deputies were mostly left-wing liberals who wanted drastic changes, including republicanism, but were firm constitutionalists. The Minister of Finance, Kokovtsov, wrote that the throne room presented 'a queer spectacle'.

The entire right side of the room was filled with uniformed people, members of the State Council and, further on, the Tsar's retinue. The left side was crowded with the members of the Duma, a small number of them had appeared in full dress, while the overwhelming majority ... occupying the first places near the throne were dressed, as if intentionally, in workers' blouses and cotton shirts, and behind them was a crowd of peasants ... some in national dress, and a multitude of the clergy.[29]

The respectable group on the right of the throne did not think much of the occasion. Afterwards, the Dowager Empress, who had struggled to keep back her tears, talked to Kokovtsov of the 'incomprehensible hatred' on the faces of the deputies. The Minister of the Interior, Peter Stolypin, whispered that he expected one of them to hurl a bomb at any moment. And the Minister of Court, Count Fredericks, declared passionately: 'The Deputies – they give one the impression of a gang of criminals who are only waiting for a signal to throw themselves upon the ministers and cut their throats. What wicked faces! I will never again set foot among those people.'[30]

3

The Birth of an Heir

Shakespeare's aphorism that beauty lies in the eye of the beholder was borne out by the courtiers surrounding the Empress. At the turn of the century Alexandra was only twenty-nine and at the height of her good looks, yet the gentlemen who later wrote their memoirs were so indifferent to her appearance that they scarcely refer to it. Count Witte, who hated her, is a notable exception and admits begrudgingly: 'Alexandra was not without physical charms.'

The ladies were more generous. Lili Dehn, whose husband was an officer on board the imperial yacht, first met the Empress in her garden at Tsarskoe Selo.

Through the masses of greenery came a tall and slender figure. . . . The Empress was dressed in white with a thin white veil draped around her hat. Her complexion was delicately fair . . . her hair reddish gold, her eyes . . . were dark blue and her figure was supple as a willow wand. I remember that her pearls were magnificent and that diamond earrings flashed coloured fires whenever she moved her hand. . . . I noticed that she spoke Russian with a strong English accent. [1]

The Empress's failure to attract, despite her fine looks, sprang from her own animosity, rooted in Victorian priggishness. She could not conceal her contempt for the rich, indolent society of St Petersburg with its scandalous loose living. Although she had lived in Russia six years, she still had not made a single friend in the capital. She disliked going there but Nicholas felt that it was his duty as sovereign to move into the Winter Palace for a few weeks every year and to take part in 'the season'. In January the sovereign always gave a ball to which the diplomatic service was invited; after that there were lunches and dinners and one or two receptions to which deserving subjects were bidden.

Since Alexandra had struck from her list the names of all those whose morals allowed room for improvement, her guests were remarkably uninspiring and her gatherings soon became famous for their dreariness. Two brilliant rivals offered a striking contrast to the dullness of the Grand Court. The Dowager Empress gave amusing parties at the Anitchkov Palace, distinguished by the best French food and wine, while Grand Duchess Marie Pavlovna, the wife of the Tsar's uncle, Grand Duke Vladimir, organized glittering balls studded with celebrities from every part of Europe.

The life of the imperial couple followed the pattern laid down by Nicholas's father, and revolved around a series of family outings, the only events that Alexandra really liked. In the early summer they went to the

OPPOSITE Alexandra and Alexis.

lovely palace at Peterhof on the Gulf of Finland; in the autumn to one of the royal hunting lodges in Poland where the Tsar shot bison and deer; before Christmas to Livadia in the sub-tropical Crimea to play tennis and swim. The Crimean estate was on a peninsula that jutted into the Black Sea and the Sea of Azov. High hills protected it from the cold winds of the north, and almost every variety of fruit and flower grew in the valleys – most spectacular were the roses climbing riotously over all the buildings. The natives were Tartars, magnificent horsemen who trotted along the dusty roads as proud and erect as centaurs. The little Grand Duchesses were always delighted to

The Tsar with Edward VII of England, on board the imperial yacht Standart. *On the left is the Duke of York, later George V.*

come here and later wrote that, whereas St Petersburg was 'duty', Livadia was 'sheer pleasure'.

Even more exciting than the visits to the Crimea, however, were the annual cruises in the imperial yacht, *Standart*. This ship was a 4,500-ton beauty that had been built for the Tsar in Denmark and was regarded by kings and millionaires as the world's most desirable yacht. Although she was as big as a small cruiser, fuelled by coal and propelled by steam, she had the graceful lines of a sailing ship and was painted an elegant black and gold. On the decks were white awnings and wicker chairs and tables; below were drawing-rooms and music-rooms and tea-rooms filled with priceless furniture. The dining-rooms were panelled in mahogany and the state rooms decorated in the Empress's favourite chintzes. Although the crew numbered over a hundred, and there were another hundred servants, the ship had so much space that she often carried a platoon of Marine Guards and an entire brass band. The *Standart* was so modern that King Edward asked the Tsar if his own British shipbuilders could study the yacht's plans.

When the imperial family was aboard, a sailor, or *diadka*, was assigned to each one of the little Grand Duchesses to look after the child's personal safety. The Empress loved the carefree life and often played the piano and sang duets with Anna Vyrubova. But what she liked best was to sit on deck, talking and sewing, her children playing nearby.

One day, in the Finnish fjords, the *Standart* came to a shuddering, crashing halt, and the yacht keeled to one side. There was a moment of panic as first thoughts always flew to bomb outrages. The Emperor and Empress ran along the decks scooping up the children, but there were no further alarms. The escort vessels took the family off the listing yacht and set sail for home.

Before the Emperor left the *Standart*, he entered the cabin of the Flag Captain, who was responsible for the safety of the imperial family, and found the man with a revolver in his hand, about to shoot himself. Nicholas persuaded the distraught captain not to do anything so foolish; and when an inquiry eventually took place it was discovered that the yacht was grounded on an uncharted rock. The captain's honour was satisfied and he thanked Nicholas for saving his life.

Although the Empress was not attractive to strangers, her home life was triumphantly successful. 'The life of their Majesties', wrote one of the ladies-in-waiting, 'was a cloudless happiness of mutual unlimited love.' 'Nicholas was much more than a loving and devoted husband,' wrote another courtier. 'He was literally the lover of his life's partner.' 'Never in all the twelve years of my association with them,' wrote Anna Vyrubova, the Tsarina's confidante, 'did I hear an important word or surprise an angry look between the Emperor and Empress.'

Apart from being a good wife and mother, Alexandra seemed to have no idea of her duties as an Empress. The notion of 'courting popularity' with the public would have struck her as incredibly vulgar. Furthermore, it would

The Empress, camera in hand (all the imperial family were keen amateur photographers), with the three eldest Grand Duchesses – Olga, Tatiana and Marie.

have run counter to her conception of autocracy, for an absolute monarch does not curry favour but issues orders. One of the ironies of the situation sprang from the fact that a young princess with an English mother, brought up by Queen Victoria who bowed to the 'Mother of Parliaments', should have become so fiercely and uncompromisingly autocratic. Alexandra, however, had received her indoctrination when she was only fourteen from her brother-in-law, the Grand Duke Serge. He had pointed out that English parliamentary rule would be disastrous in Germany and grotesque in Russia. Later these tenuous first impressions were turned into strong, inflexible beliefs by the Orthodox Church. If the Tsar was anointed by God, his will was sacred.

Alexandra did not believe that loyalty to the Tsar could be solicited by the smiles of the Tsar's wife. She, therefore, was determined to have a private life. 'She could not understand', wrote General Mossolov, the head of the Chancellery, 'how the affairs of her family could interest the whole country.

'It is my personal business" she would say again and again. "I wish people would not interfere in my affairs."'[2] Indeed, her refusal to humour the public caused endless trouble. Once, when she was expecting a baby, the imperial couple travelled to the Crimea. On leaving St Petersburg they gave orders that they did not want any receptions *en route*, or any crowds waiting in the stations. In spite of all precautions, as they came to a halt in a small, remote town, they saw that several hundred people had gathered, dressed in their Sunday clothes. The Empress at once ordered the blinds of her car to be drawn. The provincial governor was on the platform and the Court Minister urged the Tsar to come to the window, if only for a moment. He explained that the crowd had stood on the platform most of the night to catch a fleeting glimpse of their sovereign. But when the Tsar made a move toward the window the Empress stopped him, saying sternly that he had no right to encourage people 'who were not carrying out his orders'. Nevertheless, the Court Minister persisted and in the end Nicholas showed himself. The people went wild with joy but the Empress would not allow her daughters to appear and refused to lift her own blinds even a crack.

When the Dowager Empress heard of the incident she exploded angrily.

If she were not there, Nicky would be twice as popular. She is a regular German. She thinks the Imperial family should be 'above that sort of thing'. What does she mean? Above winning the people's affection? ... Nicky himself has all that is required for popular adoration; all he needs to do is to show himself to those who want to see him. How many times I have tried to make it plain to her. She won't understand; perhaps she hasn't it in her to understand. And yet, how often she complains of the public indifference towards her.[3]

The only shadow on the 'cloudless happiness' of the imperial couple was the fact that Alexandra had produced three daughters and not a single son. In 1901 she was pregnant for the fourth time and throughout the whole of the nine months prayed for an heir to the throne. When a daughter was born, Nicholas had to walk in the park to overcome his disappointment before facing his wife.

After that, Alexandra grew frantic, and began to clutch at every straw, even the supernatural. The two dark-skinned daughters of the King of Montenegro, known as the 'black pearls', were the high priestesses of the occult. During the war with Turkey these girls had been educated at the Smolny Institute in St Petersburg, as protégés of the Empress Marie Alexandrovna, and had ended up marrying Russian Grand Dukes: Nicholas Nicolaevich and his brother Peter.

In 1900, when the royal couple visited France, the Grand Duchess Militsa – Peter's wife – had brought a clairvoyant, Philippe Nazier-Vachod, into their circle. This little mild-mannered charlatan had been prosecuted twice in France for practising medicine without a licence. But the Empress was so taken with him that the Tsar obligingly adjusted the matter by commanding the Academy of Medine in St Petersburg to grant him the necessary recognition. The Empress invited Nazier-Vachod to St Petersburg and, in the company of her husband, spent hours with the Grand Duchess Militsa tipping tables. Later Nazier-Vachod conducted seances at Livadia where he endeared himself to Nicholas by relaying messages from Alexander III. One glorious day, not long after the birth of the fourth daughter, Anastasia, Nazier-Vachod told the Empress that she was *enceinte* again; he claimed to know how to control the sex of the baby, and guaranteed that it would be a boy.

All festivities were cancelled, and before long European papers were hinting at the approach of a 'happy event' in the Russian imperial family. Six months passed and the Empress had an attack of nerves. The royal physicians were called, and after an examination told Alexandra that there was no sign of a pregnancy. Without more ado, Nazier-Vachod was sent back to France.

Notwithstanding this disappointing experience, the Tsarina still clung to the Montenegrin Grand Duchesses who now advised her to seek the intercession of Seraphim, a pious old hermit who had lived and died in Sarov in 'the odour of sanctity'. All that was necessary, said Militsa, was official recognition of the hermit's saintliness. So the Procurator of the Holy Synod, still the venerable Pobedonostsev, was invited to lunch and asked to canonize Seraphim. The churchman protested that such a serious step would have to be preceded by a thorough investigation of the candidate's life. Whereupon the Empress interposed angrily that 'everything is within the Tsar's power, even to the making of saints'. In the end, the canonization ceremony took place. The Empress bathed at night in a miraculous fountain adjoining the grace; a few weeks later to her great joy she found that this time there was no doubt; she was pregnant.

The boy for whom she had longed so desperately was born on 30 July 1904, in the midst of the war with Japan. 'A great, never-to-be-forgotten day,' wrote Nicholas in his diary, 'when the mercy and blessing of God has visited us so clearly. At a quarter past one o'clock in the afternoon Alix gave birth to a son whom we have called Alexis. ....'

The joy of the mother and father was short-lived, for six weeks later Nicholas wrote apprehensively:

Alix and I have been very much worried. A haemorrhage began this morning with the slightest cause from the navel of our small Alexis. It lasted with but a few interruptions until evening. We had to call ... the surgeon Federov who at seven o'clock applied a bandage. The child was remarkably quiet and even merry, but it was a dreadful thing to have to live through such anxiety. [The next day:] This morning there again was some blood on the bandage but the bleeding stopped at noon. The child spent a quiet day and his healthy appearance somewhat quieted our anxiety.

For some months Alexandra managed to choke back her terrible fears. The child looked so healthy it was impossible to believe that he was suffering from a fatal defect. 'How beautiful he was,' explained the adoring Anna, 'how healthy, how normal, with his golden hair, his blue eyes, and his expression of intelligence so rare for a child so young.'[4]

*Princess Militsa of Montenegro married the Grand Duke Peter, and was influential
in introducing the imperial family to Rasputin and other dubious mystics.*

The Tsarevich aged about two.

As the months passed and Alexis tried to crawl, and then to walk, bumps and bruises grew to dark blue swellings as the blood beneath the skin failed to clot. There was no longer any doubt. Alexis had haemophilia.

Even today, there is still no cure for this terrible disease, transmitted by women to their male progeny.

While women carry the defective genes, they almost never suffer from the disease. With rare exceptions it strikes only males. Yet it does not necessarily strike all males in a family. . . . If the child is a girl the family cannot know with certainty whether she is a haemophilic carrier until she grows and has children of her own. The secret is locked within the structure of the chromosomes.[5]

Queen Victoria was the carrier. When she learned that her son, Leopold,

Duke of Albany, had haemophilia she protested that 'this disease is not in our family'. But it only meant that she was the first agent. Two of her daughters, Alice and Beatrice, transmitted the defective genes to their own children. One of Alice's sons, Frittie, died of a haemorrhage after an accident when he was only three, and two of Alice's daughters, Alix and Irene, had haemophiliac sons. Beatrice also had haemophiliac sons, and Beatrice's daughter, Victoria-Eugenie, who married Alfonso XIII of Spain, had two more haemophiliacs.

It is astonishing that the heirs to great thrones were allowed to marry into families afflicted by this disease, particularly as the genetic pattern was well known. It had been discovered by Dr Otto John of Philadelphia in 1803 and confirmed by Dr Christian Nasse of Bonn in 1820. In the nineteenth century medical knowledge was not so widely spread as it is today, and 'scientific facts' were not regarded as wholly reliable. Nevertheless, royalty should have received the best advice, and one can only conclude that haemophilia, because of its capriciousness, was still believed to be a dispensation of the Almighty. The fact that the blood does not clot means that it continues to flow. An apparently harmless bump that leaves the skin intact can result in a swelling the size of a melon. Internal haemorrhages almost always provoke inflammation and temperature but the worst suffering comes when the blood flows into the joints. The limbs twist and contract to make room for the infusion, and the victim screams in agony. No one knows why the haemorrhage comes to an end; sometimes it never stops and the child dies. On other occasions the sufferer recovers slowly, white and listless and unable to straighten his limbs for months at a time.

The Empress refused to accept this awful scourge. When the doctors admitted their inability to cure the disease, she decided to wring from the Almighty what science denied her. She had a private chapel built in the crypt of the Federovski Sobor, a church in the imperial park at Tsarskoe Selo used by members of the household and soldiers of the guard. Here each day, kneeling on the stone floor in the light of oil lamps, she spent hours begging for the recovery of her son, murmuring over and over, as though to reassure herself: 'God is just.'

Alexandra grieved alone. Apart from the close members of her family, only a few people at court – doctors, nannies and attendants – knew that Alexis was afflicted with haemophilia. Everyone who knew, or even suspected, was sworn to secrecy. Alexandra was determined to prevent the world from intervening in the tragedy. Not only would it weaken the dynasty, but the thought of receiving commiserations from strangers was intolerable. Even her daughters were told never to discuss their brother's illness with anyone.

The Swiss tutor, Pierre Gilliard, who arrived at the palace in 1906 to teach French to the Grand Duchesses, did not learn what was wrong with the Tsarevich for six years. At first he only saw Alexis riding his sledge over the snow, with the sailor in attendance, but as the boy grew older he got into the habit of dropping into his sisters' classroom regularly.

At times his visits would suddenly cease [wrote Gilliard]. Every time he disappeared everyone in the palace was smitten with the deepest depression. . . . The Grand Duchesses betrayed it in a mood of melancholy they tried in vain to conceal. When I asked them the cause they replied evasively. 'Alexis Nicolaevich is not well.' I knew that he was a prey to a disease . . . the nature of which no one told me.[6]

The Empress had turned it into 'a state secret'.

'You will some day have another friend like me who will speak to you of God,' Philippe Nazier-Vachod, the mystic, told the Empress before he returned to France in 1903. The Grand Duchess Militsa, who had introduced him to the sovereign's household, was not in the least abashed by the doctor's failure, and two years later brought a second 'holy man' into the life of Nicholas and Alexandra. On 1 November 1905 the Tsar wrote in his diary: 'We have got to know a man named Gregory from Tobolsk Province.' A year later Nicholas wrote: 'Gregory arrived at 6.45. He saw the children and talked to us until 7.45.' Still later: 'Militsa and Stana dined with us. They talked to us about Gregory the whole evening.'

Gregory Efimovich was the son of a peasant who at one time had been a coachman in the Imperial Mail. He was born in Pokrovskoe in western Siberia, 250 miles from the Ural mountains. Tall and strong, with burning, deep-set eyes, he won a reputation at an early age for trying to seduce every girl he met. For a while he worked as a wagoner transporting goods and passengers to other villages, which gave him new opportunities for licentiousness, and earned him the nickname of 'Rasputin' – the disreputable one. Although he could neither read nor write, he had great originality and a flair for drama that made him a superlative storyteller.

He took up farming, married and had four children. One day while he was ploughing he saw a vision and heard a voice urging him to make a pilgrimage. He walked 2,000 miles to the monastery of Mount Athos in Greece. When he returned two years later, he had a thick black beard and an aura of sanctity which seemed to be enhanced by the fact that he seldom washed. He began to bless people and look into the future for them. Gradually he began to build a reputation as a prophet.

When he visited St Petersburg in 1903, his fame travelled before him. The famous churchman Father John of Kronstadt, former private confessor of Alexander III, received Rasputin as 'a notorious *moujik* who had sinned and repented'. The second trip to the capital in 1905 was even more successful. This time the aged Archimandrite Theopanes and Bishop Hermogen of Saratov both gave him their blessing. Then the two Montenegrin Grand Duchesses made a fuss of him and finally led him to the Alexander Palace. Rasputin charmed the imperial couple by his simplicity and his quaint way of expressing himself. When he talked they thought they were hearing the authentic voice of peasant Russia – the Russia that loved the Tsar. He had no fear of them and never referred to them as 'Majesty'. He greeted them by kissing them peasant fashion and calling them *Batiushka* and *Manushka*,

Gregory Efimovich, known as Rasputin.

Father and Mother. When the children were about, he sat on the floor and told them fairy stories about the enchanted world of Siberia.

The Tsar's sister, the Grand Duchess Olga, met him for the first time at one of these family gatherings inside the palace in 1905. She recalled many years later:

They were completely at ease with him. I still remember little Alexis aged three deciding he was a rabbit, jumping up and down the room. And then, quite suddenly Rasputin caught the child's hand and led him to his bedroom, and we three followed. There was something like a hush as though we had found ourselves in Church. In Alexis' bedroom no lamps were lit, the only light came from the candles burning in front of some beautiful ikons. The child stood very still by the side of the giant, whose head was bowed. I knew he was praying. It was all most impressive. I also knew that my little nephew had joined him in prayer. . . .[7]

Olga Alexandrovna told the journalist who wrote her memoirs after the Second World War that she often saw, with her own eyes, irrefutable proof of Rasputin's healing power. Soon after her first glimpse of the *starets* Alexis fell in the garden at Tsarskoe Selo. His leg was scarcely bruised and he did not cry, but the fall had started internal bleeding.

Olga hurried to join Alexandra and found the family in a state of fearful agitation. The child had dark patches under his eyes and his leg was badly swollen.

The doctors were just useless. They looked more frightened than any of us and they kept wondering among themselves. . . . It was growing late, and I was persuaded to go to my room. Alicky then sent a message to Rasputin in St Petersburg. He reached the palace about midnight or even later. By that time I had reached my apartment, and early in the morning Alicky called me to go to Alex's room. I just could not believe my eyes. The little boy was not just alive – but well. He was sitting up in bed, the fever gone, the eyes clear and bright, not a sign of any swelling on the leg. Later I learned from Alicky that Rasputin had not even touched the child but merely stood at the foot of the bed and prayed. . . .[8]

To this day no one has been able to give a medically convincing explanation of Rasputin's power to stop the Tsarevich's haemorrhages. Was it hypnotics or some unknown form of suggestion picked up from the wandering mystics of the East? Or was the Empress right in thinking that Rasputin was 'the man of God' that Nazier-Vachod had said would come into her life? The court doctors were unable to help her son, so it is not surprising that she began to look upon the Siberian peasant as divinely inspired. His interventions always seemed to follow the same pattern. He arrived in a moment of despair and assured the parents that the boy would recover. Sometimes the next morning, sometimes twenty-four hours later, the bleeding would stop. 'Call it what you will,' said Alexis's nurse, Alexandra Tegleva, 'Rasputin could promise the Empress her boy's life while he lived.'

As Rasputin strengthened his position with the imperial family, his stays in the capital grew longer and more frequent. He never discussed the Tsarevich with anyone, but he talked freely of his visits to the palace and told how he prayed aloud with 'Mama' and 'Papa'. Before long a number of important hostesses were making a fuss over him and repeating his odd expressions and amusing metaphors. Some society ladies, on the look-out for diversion, were fascinated by his 'stable' manners; the uninhibited way he plunged his dirty hands into his favourite fish soup and talked of women as 'fillies' – 'Only too glad to serve you, my pretty one.' Some of the ladies began to shower him with money, but he was not venal, and gave it away to the needy. As for himself, he accepted only enough for his basic wants; bed and breakfast and a few silk shirts to wear at the grandest soirées.

Rasputin began by being cautious and well-behaved, but before long his sensuous nature got the better of him and he was seducing – very sanctimoniously – every woman who came near him. 'You think I am polluting you,' he would whisper, 'but I'm not, I am purifying you.' To others he would quote the Orthodox liturgy, with a slight leer: 'Let us love one another that we may profess our faith in common.' He eased the conscience of the women he slept with by presenting sin as a great virtue. True saints, he said, turn to filth so that their aureole will shine all the more brilliantly. When he got drunk, he explained that it was the only way to show the full hideousness of vice.

According to the women who surrounded Rasputin, [wrote Mossolov] anything whatever was permitted since his mission was to expose the ugliness of vice under every conceivable form. For those who rebelled against this abominable theory, he produced another precept, borrowed from monastical practice, and enlisted in the service of his lubricity. 'You have too much vainglory; you must humiliate yourself.'[9]

'The gentle but uneducated Emperor,' commented the British Ambassador, Sir Arthur Nicholson, 'is afflicted with the misfortune of being weak on every point except his own autocracy.'

The Emperor had conveniently forgotten that the granting of a constitution probably had saved his throne, and now spent his time pretending that it had never happened. Although he had approved a parliament based on a series of Fundamental Laws, it had included the sweeping declaration: 'To the Emperor of all the Russias belongs the supreme autocratic power'; and this, combined with Witte's last-minute additions, allowed him all the scope he needed to continue thinking of himself as God's anointed.

The only two parties in Russia in 1905 were the revolutionary 'SDs' and 'SRs', both of whom boycotted the election. Consequently two new parties sprang into life – the Constitutionalists, known as Cadets, and the Octobrists. Both were liberal groups led by distinguished men – an historian, Paul Miliukov, and an intrepid traveller, Alexander Guchkov, who had made himself an authority on the trouble spots of Eastern Europe. Although the new parties were resolutely opposed to Marxism, when the first session opened in the Tauride Palace their demands struck the Tsar as 're-

The young Tsarevich. ABOVE With some pet sheep, LEFT On board the Standart, *OPPOSITE ABOVE With a Sicilian donkey-cart presented to him by the King of Italy, and OPPOSITE BELOW With his father aboard the* Standart.

98

volutionary': expropriation of private land; universal suffrage; and the dismissal of all ministers appointed by the Emperor in favour of new men selected by the Duma. The government replied that these demands were 'inadmissible', and after two months of shouting and bickering the Tsar shut down the Duma.

First he dismissed the aged Ivar Goremykin and appointed Peter Stolypin as his new Prime Minister. The moment was tense with apprehension when Stolypin locked the doors of the Tauride Palace and posted notice of dissolution. No one knew what would happen and most people felt that a new outbreak of violence was inevitable. Many of the deputies fled to Finland and appealed to the people to defy the government by refusing to pay taxes or to serve in the army; but the public was too weary to respond.

A second Duma was elected in 1907, but it went the way of the first. This time the revolutionary parties had taken part in the election; and one of the deputies, Zurabov, made the mistake of declaring, quite falsely, that the army was training its men for the express purpose of suppressing civilians. He then went a step further and called on the troops to revolt. Nicholas immediately accused the assembly of 'plotting against the sovereign' and once again closed it down. Thirty Social Democratic deputies – all small fry – were exiled to Siberia, and others placed under police surveillance. The Tsar would have liked to end the experiment in constitutionalism once and for all but Stolypin insisted that a parliament was necessary. He changed the electoral laws with the result that the third Duma, composed mainly of landed gentry and conservatives, lasted its full, five-year course. Miliukov and Guchkov were again elected as heads of their respective parties. They were republicans, not monarchists, but they were firm constitutionalists and they did their best to keep their followers on an orderly path. They made the most of the 'immunity' accorded to members of the Duma and used the newly won freedom of the Press to promote their ideas.

All of them respected Stolypin, who was only forty-three when he became Chairman of the Ministers' Council, equivalent to Prime Minister. He was not a genius but he had a prodigious capacity for work and a sharp eye for detail. When he rose in the Duma he looked like a mammoth teddy bear in his frock coat with the large gold watch and chain. He had a striking black beard and a cold, even voice. Everyone admired him. 'Unlike most Russians he looked one straight in the eye,' wrote an English diplomat. 'I cannot tell you how much I have come to like and respect this man,' the Tsar wrote to his mother.

When Stolypin took office in 1906 the country was still bordering on revolution. Everywhere there was chaos and violence. During 1906 and 1907, over 1,000 police officials and *Zemstvo* administrators were murdered. Scores of manor houses were still being burned down and dozens of banks robbed to provide funds for revolutionary groups. But the anarchy was not all political. The young and adventurous, the old and bored, criminals and defectives, helped to swell the ranks. In June 1907, a group of men and women waylaid a bank coach in broad daylight and escaped with 34,000 roubles – about 50,000 dollars – but only a small proportion found its way to party leaders.

Stolypin tackled the lawlessness with vigour. He instigated drum-head courts which tried and sentenced cases within forty-eight hours. These courts became known as 'Stolypin's neckties': over 14,000 revolutionaries were hanged within the next twelve months.

One act of terror which no one in Russia bothered to investigate took place in 1906 when Father Gapon, who had led the marchers on Bloody Sunday, returned from a long trip abroad. Although the priest had joined the revolutionaries and issued flamboyant statements against the government, he had not been back a month before he fell under the spell of Ratchkovsky, a new police chief in St Petersburg. Gapon was a vain man and responded to the policeman's insistence that 'Russia has need of men like you.' If Gapon would serve the *Okhrana* and help to stop the terror, the Government would improve the conditions of the workers.

Gapon agreed and told the police all he knew about the Battle Organization of which Ievno Asev, the double agent, was still the leader. He also promised to try and persuade his friend, the engineer Rutenberg, an active terrorist, to work for the *Okhrana*. But when the priest called upon Rutenberg and offered him 25,000 roubles to betray his friends the engineer asked for time to think about it. He then informed the Battle Organization. Although Asev was on the police payroll himself, he pretended to be incensed by the duplicity and said that Gapon must be killed 'like a snake'. A few weeks later Rutenberg took Gapon to a deserted villa on the Finnish frontier to discuss the proposition. While the two men were talking, a group of revolutionaries

Stolypin dealt rigorously with revolutionary unrest, and was assassinated in 1911.

burst into their room. Gapon fell on his knees and begged for mercy, but the men silently placed a noose around his neck and attached it to an iron on the wall. A few minutes later he was dead; the police did not find the body for several months.

Perhaps Stolypin's least successful activity was his preoccupation with the *Okhrana*. He not only followed Plehve's strategy of employing double agents, but greatly increased their number. Indeed, by 1911 it was estimated that one tenth of all revolutionary groups were composed of police informers. This policy had its drawbacks, for no one could be sure which side anyone was really on. It also spread the practice of treachery through the whole fabric of society by giving it an aura of respectability. The British journalist, Dr Dillon, felt that unless someone tried to inject a sense of honour into the Byzantine love of deceit, Russia would become ungovernable. 'In that connivance at lawlessness', he wrote in May 1905, 'lurks a danger the insidiousness of which few people realize.'

Most double agents connived at lawlessness, but Stolypin valued their services, and was confident that he could control them. He knew that Asev was on his payroll and even suspected that the latter had organized the assassinations of Plehve and the Grand Duke Serge. Although several years later he, too, was murdered by one of his own police agents, in 1906 he was full of confidence. He worked closely with Gerassimov, whom he had appointed as chief of the *Okhrana*, and even approved a plan that concerned his own safety. Gerassimov suggested destroying the Battle Organization by demoralization. Asev would excite his comrades by undertaking the assassination of Stolypin, but every attempt would meet with failure until the participants drifted away in frustration and disgust.

Unfortunately the *Okhrana* plan was spectacularly unsuccessful. After repeated disappointments, Asev's colleagues decided to have a try on their own. Without telling their chief, they formed a small group, the Maximalists, and went to Stolypin's house at the hour when he received official callers. The guard refused to let them pass beyond the hall, so they threw their bombs where they stood. The explosions killed the guards, the terrorists, and twenty or thirty visitors, and demolished the greater part of the villa. Stolypin's small children were badly injured but the Prime Minister was working in his study and escaped covered with ink, but without a scratch.

When Asev heard the news he was so frightened that Stolypin would hold him responsible that he forced the Battle Organization to issue a statement deploring 'the methods of the Maximalists'. Since their methods were no different from the methods of other terrorists, his comrades were puzzled. Asev's nerves were so shattered that eighteen months later he left Russia for good, and settled down in Berlin. He had amassed plenty of money and became a respectable stockbroker under the name Alexander Neumayer. When the world war broke out, however, he was imprisoned as a revolutionary and died a few months after being released in 1917.

In 1908, as home affairs improved, foreign affairs began to cause the Emperor great anxiety. In the Balkans the rivalry between Austria and Russia had lain in abeyance for many years because of Russia's preoccupations in the Far East. But not long after the Portsmouth Peace Treaty, Nicholas II had appointed a new Foreign Minister, Alexander Izvolsky, a professional diplomat. Izvolsky looked like a stage villain. Vain and ambitious, he

Izvolsky (right) on board the German imperial yacht Hohenzollern
in 1908, with the German Chancellor von Bülow.

'strutted on little lacquered feet ... wore a pearl pin, an eye glass, white spats and ... left behind him, as he passed onwards, a slight scent of *violette de parme*'.

The villainy was not only in the looks, for Izvolsky's ambition was served by cowardice and treachery, and a determination to use any means to gain his end. He was not in the least discouraged by the fact that Europe was now neatly divided into two camps – the Triple Alliance consisting of Germany, Austria–Hungary and a doubtful Italy, and the Triple Entente consisting of Russia, France and an even more doubtful Britain. Although all these great powers were enlarging their armies and increasing their armaments, any number of cross-currents swept the two groups. England and France had no quarrel with Austria, but feared Germany; Russia, on the other hand, got on reasonably well with Germany but regarded Austria–Hungary as an intolerable obstacle to Panslav ambitions in the Balkans.

Izvolsky decided to end the Austro–Russian stalemate by sweeping the pieces from the board and starting the game afresh. At a secret ministerial council in February 1908 he told the Tsar that Russia could not afford to remain a passive spectator. If she allowed the Balkan Question to remain indefinitely 'on ice' she would lose 'the fruits of her century-long efforts, ceasing to play the role of a great power, and falling into the position of a second-rate State to which no one pays any attention'.[10] Nicholas II minuted this paper: 'God helps those who help themselves.'

Izvolsky was not contemplating force. Russia was too weak for that. He was thinking of a deal with Austria which would result in a glorious Russian coup and delight the Tsar by making up for the ignominious defeat at the hands of Japan. Indeed, he had already dropped a hint in the ear of the Austrian Foreign Secretary and had been pleased by the reaction. 'Russia', he told Baron von Aehrenthal, 'has lost Manchuria and Port Arthur and thereby access to the sea in the East. The main point for Russia's military and naval expansion of power lies henceforth in the Black Sea. From there Russia must gain an access to the Mediterranean.'[11]

In the summer of 1908 Izvolsky was even more explicit. The 'Young Turks' had seized power in Constantinople and the country was in a state of disorganization; the time had come to act. He sent an *aide memoire* to Baron von Aehrenthal proposing that Russia should settle the Straits Question by securing the right to send Russian warships through the Bosphorus and the Dardanelles; Austria, in return, could strengthen her position in Bosnia and Herzegovina by converting her thirty-year-old occupation into a direct annexation. Although both these moves would constitute an infringement of the Berlin Treaty of 1878, Izvolsky was convinced that an agreement between Russia and Austria would pacify the Great Powers.

The Emperor was delighted with Izvolsky's plan, since he had always longed to see Russian warships moving through the Straits. Perhaps it was not astonishing, but at least it was surprising, that both the sovereign and his Foreign Secretary were wholly out of touch with Russian opinion. The question of the Straits had been receding into the background over the past decade, while the idea of a Federated Slavdom, once under Bulgaria but now under the leadership of Serbia, had been gaining adherents. The most vociferous exponents of Russian Panslavism were the two Montenegrin princesses, Anastasia and Militsa, who had introduced Rasputin to the Empress. Anastasia was the wife of the Grand Duke Nicholas Nicolaevich, destined to become commander-in-chief of the Russian army at the outbreak of war, while Militsa was married to his brother, the Grand Duke Peter. A third sister, the wife of Peter Karageorgevich, King of Serbia, completed the magic circle. These powerful influences promoted the idea of a Greater Serbia which would be closely allied to Montenegro and would include Bosnia and Herzegovina and perhaps a slice of Macedonia.

Izvolsky's bland suggestion, therefore, ran completely counter to current opinion. The Russian minister was in France when Austria announced the annexation. Izvolsky dealt firmly with the Serbian Legation in Paris which fell into an immediate uproar. 'You Serbians surely cannot be thinking of driving Austria–Hungary out of Bosnia and Herzegovina by force of arms. And we Russians, on the other hand, cannot wage war on Austria on account of these provinces. . . . I have foreseen this step . . . and it did not surprise me. . . .'[12]

Izvolsky reached London to find the British government steaming with anger over Austria's high-handed breach of the Berlin Treaty. Although, as far as Russia was concerned, the British Foreign Secretary was all smiles, things did not go as he expected. Of course, Sir Edward Grey assured him, he understood Russia's desire for a free passage through the Straits; he regarded it as 'fair and reasonable' and was not against it 'in principle'. Nevertheless, it could not be a one-sided arrangement; if the Straits were opened to Russia they would have to be opened to all the powers. This, of course, was the last thing that Izvolsky intended. Freedom of the Straits meant Russian warships; not foreign warships which might sail into the Black Sea and bomb Odessa. Izvolsky argued, implored, threatened and wept but the British were adamant.

Meanwhile a wave of indignation was sweeping Russia. The Foreign Minister had made a complete fool of himself; he had been duped by von Aehrenthal, and even if his plan had succeeded, were the Straits worth the sacrifice of Bosnia and Herzegovina? After all, these two provinces had been selected to form the core of Greater Serbia, Russia's springboard into the Balkans. Unanimously the press accused Izvolsky of swopping the provinces for 'a mess of pottage'; and some papers asked sarcastically why he was so concerned to open the Straits to Russian warships when most of them, thanks to the Japanese Navy, were laying at the bottom of the sea.

Izvolsky saw the spectre of a shattered career arising before him; disgrace, ridicule, ruin. So he began to lie. He regaled everyone who would listen, including Edward VII, with accounts of Baron von Aehrenthal's 'duplicity'. He flatly denied that he had concluded a bargain, insisting that he had

The imperial family were very close to each other. LEFT Anastasia sewing, BELOW The room where the children had their music lessons at Tsarskoe Selo, OPPOSITE ABOVE The Tsarina with her children, and OPPOSITE BELOW The imperial family on the Hohenzollern.

expected Austria's annexation claims to be placed before a conference of the powers. He had been double-crossed by von Aehrenthal's premature announcement, and he referred to the Foreign Secretary as a 'half-Jew' and 'certainly no gentleman'. The British Foreign Office knew perfectly well that he was lying, but Sir Edward Grey decided: 'We must do our best to support him, such as he is.' As a result King Edward wrote to the Tsar praising Izvolsky. 'You know how anxious I am for the most friendly relations between Russia and England ... and I feel confident that through your M. Izvolsky these hopes will be realized. ...'[13]

Izvolsky was saved but Bosnia and Herzegovina appeared to be lost. Nowhere was the excitement greater than in Serbia. The small kingdom behaved as though its own territory had been invaded. War credits were voted; mobilization plans drawn up; irregular armed bands formed; a National Defence Society established. From the emotions aroused one might have supposed that Russia and Serbia had some prior claim to Bosnia and Herzegovina. Since Austria had been occupying and administering the provinces for years, the opposite was true. Indeed the people living in the provinces made no protest, for the transaction merely seemed to be a switch from *de facto* to *de jure* occupation. But what made the turmoil even more ludicrous was the fact that Russia more than once had affirmed Austria's right of annexation. Apparently Nicholas II was ignorant of these proceedings. '... there is something else which is really most distressing and which I had no idea of until now,' he wrote to his mother in March 1908. 'The other day Chirekoff [Charykov, Russian Ambassador in Constantinople] sent me some secret papers dating back to the Berlin Congress in 1878. It appears from them that, after endless controversy, Russia consented to a possible future annexation of Bosnia and Herzegovina. ... What an awkward situation! ... and what an embarrassing position we are in.'[14]

When Austria responded to Belgrade's belligerence by sending troops to the Serbian frontier, the German Kaiser, Wilhelm II, was alarmed. He had known nothing of Austria's annexation plan and had been furious when Vienna had announced the *fait accompli* without consulting Berlin. So he stepped in and confronted Russia and Serbia with a mediation proposal that had the ring of an ultimatum; acceptance of the annexation with no further delays; yes or no, otherwise Germany would draw back and allow Austria to deal with Serbia on her own. Affirmative answers arrived within twenty-four hours and the Tsar wired the Kaiser thanking him for preserving the peace. 'There is no doubt whatever', the head of the British Foreign Office wrote to Edward VII, 'that Aehrenthal has in his pocket a paper in which Izvolsky ... had promised to recognize the annexation of Bosnia, provided that Austria would agree to the opening of the Dardanelles ... and it is the threat of this document which has made him cave in in such an ignominious manner to the Germans. He is a very unscrupulous and unreliable man.'[15]

Izvolsky was an adept at twisting and turning, and he now presented the whole affair as a deliberate Austro–German plot to subjugate Slavdom. Soon the impressionable Tsar had swallowed Izvolsky's explanations and looked upon the mediation proposal as a harsh ultimatum. 'Once the matter had been put as definitely and unequivocally,' he wrote to his mother in March 1909, 'there was nothing for it, but to swallow one's pride and agree. . . . But our public . . . go on abusing and reviling poor Izvolsky.'[16]

'Poor Izvolsky' not only succeeded in deceiving the Tsar but the British Ambassador, Sir Arthur Nicholson, as well. 'My firm opinion', Sir Arthur wrote to a friend, 'is that both Germany and Austria are carrying out a line of policy and action carefully prepared. . . .' Many years later Sir Arthur's son and biographer explained, 'Nicholson was not at the time aware of the blackmail being applied [by Austria], and quite sincerely believed that Russia was being faced by an ultimatum. It is possible that Izvolsky exaggerated the German action in order to distract attention from his own secret commitments to Austria.'[17]

Nicholas II won great praise for his sagacity in choosing Peter Stolypin as his Prime Minister. It was the best appointment he made, for Stolypin was not only astute but lucky. During the five years of his premiership Russia had the best harvests in the whole of its history. The country relied on the export of grain, so everyone prospered, and between 1906 and 1911 industrial productivity increased by 125 per cent. Even more important, the bumper harvests helped the Prime Minister to achieve his greatest piece of legislation – the Land Reform Act. Most peasants were members of village communes and could earn their living only as part of a group. Stolypin overthrew this inefficient system and introduced the concept of private enterprise. He passed a decree enabling peasants to opt out of the commune and to claim a share of the land for themselves; he also brought large tracts of new land under cultivation, mainly in Siberia. By 1911 the country had over nine million peasant farmers.

The improvement in Russian life dealt a severe blow to the Emperor's most dangerous adversary, the revolutionary movement. None of the leaders, except Trotsky, had played any part in the upheaval of 1905. Most of them lived in exile and refused to return to Russia for fear of being arrested. Furthermore, the sharp differences between Lenin and Plekhanov had left the Social Democrats weak and divided.

The sharpest disagreement centred around Lenin's 'expropriations', known as 'exes'. He had introduced the idea of robbing banks and government offices to provide money for the party. The terrorists did not carry out the raids themselves, but hired professional thieves. In 1906 over 800,000 roubles were stolen from the Bank for Mutual Mercantile Credit in Moscow. The following year another sensational coup took place in Tiflis. A small group of men and women – among them a novice later known as Stalin – waylaid a bank coach in broad daylight and got away with 340,000 roubles. In almost all these robberies, bombs were thrown in crowded streets, taking a terrible toll of human life; but Lenin put forward his stock argument about the ends justifying the means.

Plekhanov rebelled against Lenin's 'dirty money', and in 1906 called a conference in Stockholm which voted decisively against expropriations. Lenin pretended to accept the decision but organized the raids on the sly, and pocketed the money to further his own aims. A year later Plekhanov called another conference, this time in London, hoping to heal the breach between Bolsheviks and Mensheviks. Over 300 delegates arrived, the greatest assembly of revolutionary talent – and the oddest – ever to meet. Some were dressed in frock coats and top hats, others in sheepskin hats and workers' blouses; and almost all of them had enormous beards, as a form of disguise.

Lenin arrived with a new group of followers, many of whom were destined to play a leading part in the revolution. Kamenev and Zinoviev were unknown young men who had been active in the 1905 uprising; also present were Litvinov, the future Commissar for Foreign Affairs, Voroshilov, the future Field Marshal, Rykov, Nogin, Yaroslavsky, and a supporter from Georgia, Joseph Djugashvili, who had not yet started to use the pseudonym Stalin.

Although Lenin narrowly won the vote for the party chairmanship, the conference broke up with none of the major issues settled. The truth was that the Mensheviks favoured evolutionary means to achieve the revolution, while Lenin preferred force. The Mensheviks would have liked to co-operate with the Duma, and to win power by argument and consent, but Lenin insisted that the movement must continue to work in the dark shadows of the underground.

Joseph Djugashvili, later known as Stalin, in 1906.

In 1911 he reached the nadir of his career. Two years earlier the Mensheviks had discovered that he was continuing his policy of expropriations and pocketing the money to further his own ends. They were so angry that they forced him to close down his newspaper, *Proletarii*. 'We have no party at all,' his wife observed glumly. Soon it was even worse: no party, no money, no newspaper, no following. In 1909 Marx's daughter and son-in-law, Laura and Paul Lafargues, despaired of ever seeing the revolution and committed suicide. Lenin said grimly: 'If one cannot work for the party any longer one must be able to look truth in the face and die as the Lafargues did.'

The Tsar's ministers did not find the sovereign easy to serve. His large, kindly blue eyes and his unaffected manner drew foreigners to him and impressed them with his charm. Yet Nicholas was much more than agreeable; he was devious, fitful and at times quite incalculable. Count Witte never forgot the way in which the sovereign dismissed him from his post as Chairman of the Council of Ministers. 'Our Tsar is an Oriental, a full-blooded Byzantine,' he railed. 'We talked for two solid hours. He shook my hand. He embraced me. He wished me all the luck in the world. I returned home beside myself with happiness and found a written order for my dismissal lying on the desk.'[18]

Occasionally the Emperor's fickleness stemmed from a genuine inability to maintain a point of view. He had no real will, therefore his change of mind sprang from more complicated sources. Once, when Stolypin had spent several weeks working out a programme of reform, he received a note from the Emperor congratulating him on his 'most convincing arguments', but cancelling the project.

An inner voice, [explained the Tsar] keeps on insisting ... that I do not accept responsibility for it. So far my conscience has not deceived me. Therefore I intend ... to follow its dictates. I know that you, too, believe that a Tsar's heart is in God's hands. Let it be so. For all laws established by me I bear a great responsibility before God, and I am ready to answer ... at any time.[19]

The Emperor was as profoundly religious as the Empress, but it affected him in a different way. Rather than struggle against the tribulations that overtook him, as the Empress did, he was inclined to accept every disaster as 'God's Will'. Once, when the revolution was imminent, his cousin, the Grand Duke Alexander, reproached him for his unnatural submission. 'Who, in Heaven's name, Nicky, has taught you this unique way of worshipping your God? Do you call it Christianity? No, Nicky, it sounds more like the Mohammedan fatalism of a Turkish soldier who is not afraid of death because the wide open gates of Paradise are awaiting his arrival in the Great Beyond. True Christianity, Nicky, means Action even more than it does Prayer.' 'God's Will shall be fulfilled,' Nicholas II repeated slowly. 'I was born on May sixth, the day of Job the Sufferer. I am ready to accept my doom.'[20]

The Empress was anything but complacent. She vehemently refused to accept any blight – even haemophilia – as final. She believed in miracles. She was certain that if she prayed hard enough the adversity would be overcome. On several occasions the Tsarevich's tutor, Pierre Gilliard, witnessed her unconquerable optimism. Whenever her son came into the room laughing or into the house from out-of-doors with red cheeks and sparkling eyes, she jumped to the conclusion that a miracle had taken place. 'Her heart would fill with an immense hope,' wrote Gilliard, 'and she would say: "God has heard me. He has pitied my sorrow at last."'[21]

Nicholas was aware that Alexandra's faith was quite literally the breath of life to her. When she gave her complete trust to Rasputin – a trust that was unswerving and militant – he feared that if he undermined or destroyed it, he would kill the spirit that sustained her. So he, too, resolutely refused to be 'enlightened' by ministers, friends or relations. This was unfortunate, since Rasputin's behaviour throughout 1911 was notoriously disgraceful. He seemed to throw all discretion to the wind, and when he was drunk boasted about his relationship with the imperial family. 'Mama', he said, couldn't breathe without him, and 'Papa' had fallen on his knees and said: 'You are Christ'. Almost every night some exalted lady spent the night at Rasputin's flat, and every week or so he went to the islands, where the gipsies sang and danced, and took part in wild orgies. The two bishops who had sponsored Rasputin originally were horrified by accounts of his behaviour – particularly by the scandalous allegation, later proved true, that he had raped a nun. Both of them made the mistake of going to the palace to open the Empress's eyes. She listened grimly as the Archimandrite Theopanes, Rector of the Theological College of St Petersburg, made his report, but a week later he found himself transferred to the Crimea. Bishop Hermogen of Saratov was even unluckier. He was ordered 'to the seclusion of a monastery'.

Later a monk named Illiodor also became involved in the Rasputin scandal. At one time he had been on friendly terms with the *starets* and had even visited the latter's house in Siberia. Here Rasputin had shown him shirts embroidered by the Empress, and letters written by the Tsarevich and the Grand Duchesses. He also let him read one or two extraordinary epistles from the Empress which he told Illiodor to keep if he liked.

When tales of Rasputin's licentiousness began to circulate in the Duma, Stolypin felt that it was his duty to warn the Emperor. The secret police presented him with voluminous files, which were monotonous in their repetitiveness. 'He returned at three o'clock in the morning completely drunk'; 'On the night of the twenty-fifth/sixth the actress V. spent the night with Rasputin'; 'He arrived with the Princess D. at the Royal Astoria'; 'Rasputin came home with Princess Sh. very drunk.' On this evidence Stolypin ordered Rasputin to leave the capital. The *starets* was forced to obey, but before he left he told the Empress that the police were circulating outrageous lies about him. The Empress defended him hotly to her husband, with words that ran through her letters for many years. 'Saints are always calumniated'; 'They hate him because we love him'; and as for the alleged

The wealthy and well-connected flocked around Rasputin,
who entertained them in his apartment.

debauchery, 'They accuse Rasputin of kissing women – read the apostles; they kissed everybody as a form of greeting.'[22]

The Empress's sudden hatred for Stolypin became apparent in September 1911 when the Prime Minister went to Kiev accompanied by his colleague Kokovtsov, the Minister of Finance, to attend the unveiling of a statue of Alexander III. As the procession wound through the streets the Emperor was surrounded by soldiers and police but the carriage of Stolypin and Kokovtsov was left unguarded. 'You see we are superfluous,' the Prime Minister remarked caustically. Standing in the crowd was Rasputin, who had been summoned from Siberia and brought to Kiev by Anna Vyrobuva. As Stolypin's carriage passed the *starets* waved his arms in excitement and shouted: 'Death is after him! Death is driving after him!'[23]

The next night Stolypin went to the Kiev Opera House to see Rimsky-Korsakov's *Tsar Sultan*. The Emperor and two of his daughters were in a box overlooking the stage and the audience below him sparkled with jewels and medals. In the second intermission the Prime Minister, who was sitting in the front row, rose and turned his back to the stage. A young man in evening clothes walked down the aisle toward him. A foot away he pulled out a Browning revolver and fired two shots into Stolypin's chest.

The Emperor wrote to his mother:

Olga and Tatiana were with us. During the second interval, we had just left the box as it was so hot, when we heard two sounds as though something had dropped. I thought an opera glass might have fallen on somebody's head and ran back to the box to look. To the right I saw a group of officers and other people. They seemed to be dragging someone along. Women were shrieking and directly in front of me in the stalls Stolypin was standing. He slowly turned his head toward me and with his left hand made the sign of the cross in the air. Only then did I notice that he was very pale and that his right hand and uniform were blood-stained. He slowly sank into his chair and began to unbutton his tunic. Frederick ... helped him. Olga and Tatiana ... saw what happened.[24]

Ironically Stolypin was murdered by one of his own *agents provocateurs*. The assassin's name was Mordika Bogrov, in this case clearly more active as a revolutionary than as a police informer. Bogrov had played the usual game of treachery. Before the imperial party arrived in Kiev he had told the police that he had heard of a plot to murder Stolypin. To enable him to point out the villain who might have slipped through the police net, he was given a special ticket of admittance.

Stolypin lived for five days. On the second day there was a memorial service for his recovery but not a single member of the royal family attended it. After his death Nicholas went to the nursing home and was present at a service organized by Stolypin's widow.

The Minister of Finance, Kokovtsov, was asked to assume the additional burden of the prime ministership. He was deeply shocked by the imperial couple's indifference to a great man who had served Russia with such devotion and success. 'A month after Stolypin's death,' he wrote bitterly, 'he was spoken of with perfect calm ... he was profoundly criticized and hardly a soul expressed a word of sorrow that he had gone.'

The Empress seized the opportunity to reveal her animosity still further. 'Life continually assumes new forms,' she told Kokovtsov, 'and you must not try to follow blindly the work of your predecessor. ... Find support in the confidence of the Tsar – the Lord will help you. I am sure that Stolypin died to make room for you, and all this is for the good of Russia.'[25]

The Duma was fascinated by tales of Rasputin's lascivious behaviour coupled with stories of the welcome he received from the occupants of the Alexander Palace. Up till now only a few people had been aware of Rasputin and even fewer of his influence with the sovereign. Now the stories poured out, exaggerated and often apocryphal. Since the Duma was more a talking shop than a parliament the deputies at last had something interesting to fasten on, and chattered endlessly about the mystically-minded Tsarina and the physically-minded *starets*. The third Duma had been elected in 1907 by a crippled suffrage, designed by Stolypin to give the main voting power to the landed gentry. As a result the majority party consisted of Octobrists, a conservative reform group numbering 157 members and led by Alexander Guchkov. To their right were nationalists and reactionaries, numbering 139;

and to their left fifty Cadets led by the historian Miliukov, twenty Marxist Social Democrats, a few non-Marxist Labour members, and a handful of Poles.

The outstanding personality of the Duma was Guchkov, a dashing figure straight out of the pages of *The Three Musketeers*. Grandson of a serf, and son of a prosperous Moscow merchant, Guchkov was an intrepid spirit who had taken part in the skirmishes and revolts in Macedonia and Armenia, had ridden along the Great Wall of China at the time of the Boxer Rebellion, and fought with the Boers in the South African War. By 1912, when the third Duma was drawing to the end of its five-year term, Guchkov's party had moved a long way to the left. The Octobrists had become increasingly critical of the Tsar's retention of so many of his autocratic powers. Half of them would have liked a constitutional monarchy, the other half a republic.

Under these circumstances it is not surprising that when gossip about Rasputin's debauchery came to Guchkov's ears he made the most of it. In his newspaper *The Voice of Moscow* he referred to 'that cunning conspirator against our Holy Church, that fornicator of human souls and minds . . . how much longer will the Synod remain silent and inactive in the face of this shameful comedy?'[26]

Guchkov's attack did not escape the notice of the monk, Illiodor, who by now had run into trouble with both the Church and the Empress. He was banished to a monastery, but before he went he sent Guchkov one of the letters that the Empress was alleged to have written to Rasputin. Guchkov had it hectographed and circulated, in the hundreds, throughout the capital.

My beloved, unforgettable teacher, redeemer and mentor. How tiresome it is without you! My soul is quiet and I relax only when you, my teacher, are sitting beside me. I kiss your hands and lean my head on your blessed shoulder. Oh how light, how light do I feel then. I only wish one thing: to fall asleep, forever on your shoulders and in your arms. What happiness to feel your presence near me. Where are you? Where have you gone? Oh I am so sad and my heart is longing. . . . Will you soon be again close to me? Come quickly. I am asking for your holy blessing and I am kissing your blessed hands. I love you forever. Yours, M. [Mama].[27]

Not surprisingly this letter, 'which a cynical reader might interpret as an admission of personal attraction', caused a minor sensation, and formed the basis of most of the calumnies that arose during the war. However, Illiodor was wild and unbalanced, and more sophisticated people, including Prime Minister Kokovtsov and Minister of the Interior Makarov, were convinced that Alexandra's letters were not genuine. 'We believed that the letters were apocryphal and . . . circulated for the purpose of undermining the position of the Sovereign,' wrote Kokovtsov. The two men, therefore, were determined to track down the original documents. Within a few weeks they traced the letters to the house of one of Illiodor's friends, and found no difficulty in obtaining possession of them.

When Makarov was received by the Tsar, wrote Kokovtsov, he told His Majesty the story of the letters and placed in his hands the envelope containing them. 'The Tsar turned pale, nervously took the letters from the envelope and, glancing at the Empress's handwriting, said: "Yes, this is not a counterfeit letter". Then opened a drawer of his desk and threw the letter inside, with a sharp gesture quite unusual with him.'[28]

The publication of the Empress's letter triggered off a stream of abuse concerning both the Empress and Rasputin. Nothing was said openly: everything was veiled beneath words such as 'dark forces', 'crazy piety' and 'dissolute habits'. Nevertheless the Tsar was so upset by what he termed 'attacks on his wife's honour' that he summoned General Mossolov, head of the Court Chancellery, and demanded that he put a stop to the lying insinuations. Mossolov wrote:

Their Majesties recognized freedom of speech but not freedom of publication. . . . The censorship of articles relating to the Court was my responsibility. But what could I do? . . . Articles in which no member of the Imperial family was mentioned by name were, under the very precise text of the law, not liable to be submitted at all to the censorship of the Court. That made me completely helpless.[29]

Needless to say, the Empress never forgave Guchkov. 'Hanging is too good for him,' she said. Later, 'Could not a strong railway accident be arranged in which he alone would suffer?' And again, 'Guchkov is very ill – wish he would go – it's not a sinful wish.'

OPPOSITE The Winter Palace.

4

The Scandal of Rasputin

OPPOSITE *The superb Jordan staircase in the Winter Palace.*

The Dowager Empress sent for the new Prime Minister, Kokovtsov, and told him how upset she was by Rasputin's notoriety. 'My poor daughter-in-law,' she said with tears in her eyes, 'does not perceive that she is ruining both the dynasty and herself. She sincerely believes in the holiness of an adventurer, and we are powerless to ward off the misfortune which is sure to come.'[1]

The young Empress angrily refused to send Rasputin away. Nevertheless she was disgusted by the scurrilous allegations involving herself, and began to employ a third party to carry messages and to arrange appointments with Rasputin. Although the palace swarmed with secret police and every movement and meeting was noted and recorded, Alexandra felt that she was achieving a small degree of privacy through the help of her one and only confidante, the dumpy, blonde-haired Anna Vyrubova. This lady was twelve years younger than the Empress. She was not beautiful, nor was she clever or important; yet she was destined to win a permanent, if somewhat dubious, place in the annals of history. The truth was that she was an adoring slave who loved everything that Alexandra loved, including Rasputin. Anna was too limited to exert any influence on the imperial family, yet when the revolution threatened the fact that she was a link between the Emperor and Rasputin gave her notoriety out of all proportion to the sycophantic role she played.

Anna was the daughter of Alexander Taneyev, a noted composer and Chief of the Emperor's Personal Chancellery. He lived on an estate in Moscow and Anna first met the Empress at the home of the Grand Duchess Ella. In 1901, when she was only seventeen, she nearly died of typhus and Alexandra visited her sick-bed. The young girl was so overwhelmed by this kindness that she developed a passionate admiration for Alexandra which never left her. Two years later Anna received the *chiffre* of court rank, and in 1905 she was appointed to the personal suite of the Empress.

The friendship did not develop into a deep and lasting attachment for another two years; at that time Anna was having grave doubts about her engagement to Lieutenant Boris Vyrubov. Her mystical leanings prompted her to ask the Grand Duchess Militsa to arrange a meeting for her with a holy seer whose reputation was spreading – Rasputin. The latter told her bluntly that the marriage would not last, but the Empress reminded her that she had given her word, and the ceremony took place in the presence of the sovereigns. Anna soon discovered, however, that the lieutenant had been shell-shocked at the Battle of Tsushima and was mentally unbalanced. Furthermore, he could not consummate the union. With the Empress's encouragement Anna moved into one of the imperial cottages at Tsarskoe Selo only a stone's throw from the Alexander Palace.

Nicholas and Alexandra at Spala, 1912, where Rasputin telegraphed
assuring them that the Tsarevich would live.

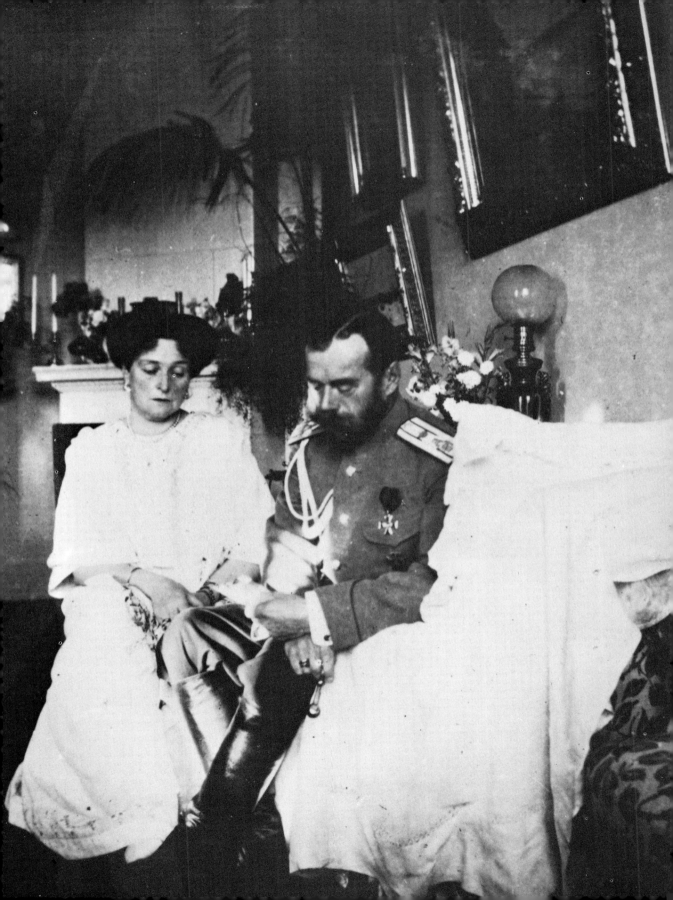

*The Tsar (right), three of the Grand Duchesses, and an unknown friend playing games.
The woman standing above them is probably Anna Vyrubova.*

The Empress blamed herself for Anna's misfortune and that summer invited her on a cruise on the royal yacht *Standart*. As the vessel sailed through Finnish waters, Anna poured out her heart and Alexandra responded by recalling her own loneliness when she first came to Russia and the unfriendliness of the disagreeable ladies who surrounded the Dowager Empress. After the trip the Empress said: 'I thank God for at last sending me a true friend.' Later that year the friend was allowed to obtain a divorce.

Anna was always an easy companion, never presumptuous and amenable to any topic of conversation. She was not interested in politics and was as much at home with children as adults. The simplest pleasures interested her.

She liked puzzles and games and could spend hours sticking photographs into albums, but what she treasured most was to be present when the Emperor read aloud in the evenings. The Empress, on the other hand, loved playing four-handed piano duets with Anna – Bach, Beethoven, Tchaikovsky. Since their voices were soprano and contralto they often sang together, and for a time took singing lessons. Both were good needlewomen and spent many afternoons sewing and embroidering. If several days passed without the Empress calling for Anna, the girl would pout; but Alexandra only laughed and called her 'our big baby' or 'our little daughter'. Sometimes, in the evening, the Tsar and Tsarina walked to Anna's cottage. It was very cold since it had been built without foundations and the damp came through the floors. 'We used to sit around the table with our legs drawn up so as to avoid contact with the cold floor,' wrote Anna. 'Their Majesties regarded my primitive way of life from the humourous side. Sitting before the blazing hearth, we drank our tea and ate little roasted cracknels, handed around by my servants. . . . I remember the Emperor once laughingly saying to me that, after such an evening, nothing but a hot bath could make him warm again.'[2]

The Empress supervised every detail of her children's education and sometimes spent hours in the schoolrooms. Apparently the four girls were rather unusual, for they never quarrelled with each other and always did what their parents told them. They were allowed to choose their own patterns for dresses, and as they grew older were allowed to invite the young officers in the neighbourhood to tennis matches and tea parties. But they longed desperately for girl friends, whom they were not allowed to have. 'The Empress dreaded for her daughters', wrote Anna, 'the companionship of over-sophisticated young women of the aristocracy whose minds, even in the schoolroom, were fed with the foolish and often vicious gossip of a decadent society. The Empress even discouraged association with cousins and near relatives, many of whom were unwholesomely precocious in their outlook of life.'[3]

The Empress's decisions on her son's activities were even more difficult. She did not dare allow boys of his own age to play with him for fear they would prove too rough. When he was five he was put in the care of a burly sailor, Derevenko. Sometimes the latter brought his own small sons to play with the Tsarevich and carefully supervised their games. But for the most part the boy was alone, guarded by the sailor every minute of the day. Sometimes Derevenko was called upon to try and alleviate the child's pain. 'I can still', wrote Anna '. . . hear the plaintive, suffering voice of Alexis begging the big sailor to "lift my arm", "put my leg up", "warm my hands" and I can see the patient, calm-eyed man working for hours on end to give the maximum of comfort to the little, pain-racked limbs.'[4]

When Pierre Gilliard became tutor to the Tsarevich, who was then eight years old, he felt that the sailor Derevenko's constant supervision might deprive the boy of all resourcefulness. He passed on his fears to the imperial couple who, to his great surprise, agreed to alter their son's routine regardless of the risk involved. At first everything went well; and then, suddenly, when the boy was standing on a chair, he fell and knocked his knee. The next day he could not walk; and the day after a large swelling had formed beneath the knee and spread down the whole leg. Gilliard wrote:

I was thunderstruck, yet neither the Tsar nor the Tsarina blamed me in the slightest. . . . The Tsarina was at her son's bedside from the first onset of the attack . . . the Tsar came the moment he was free. He tried to comfort and amuse the boy but the pain was stronger than his mother's caresses or his father's stories and moans and tears began once more. Every now and then the door opened and one of the Grand Duchesses came in on tip-toe and kissed her little brother. . . .[5]

As the months passed the Empress suffered increasingly from ill health and was glad to have Anna around to run errands for her and to deluge her with small kindnesses. When Alexis was ill she sat by his bed night after night, but when the danger passed she lay prostrate on her bed for days on end. In 1908, when Alexis was four, she began to suffer from shortness of breath which was diagnosed as 'an enlarged heart'. But even then people close to her felt that her illness was mental; psychosomatic, as it would be called today. The strain of watching her son suffering pain comparable to medieval torture had shattered her nervous system and turned her into an invalid.

She spent most of her days lying on her *chaise longue* in her boudoir – a room decorated entirely in mauve; chintz curtains with mauve flowers, carpets with mauve borders, walls and cushions and stools and eiderdowns all of mauve. 'I have been ill nearly all the time,' she wrote to her former tutor, Miss Jackson. And to her sister, Princess Victoria of Battenberg, 'Don't think my ill health depresses me personally. I don't care except to see my dear ones suffer on my account and that I cannot fulfill my duties. But once God sends such a cross it must be borne. . . .'

Nicholas, however, was frantic with worry. 'I would do anything,' he once said to Anna, 'even to going to prison if she could only be well again.' To his mother he wrote in 1910, 'She keeps to her bed most of the day, does not receive anyone, does not come out to lunches and remains on the balcony day after day. Botkin has persuaded her to go to Nauheim for a cure in the early autumn. It is very important for her to get better, for her own sake, and the children's and mine. I am completely run down mentally by worrying over her health.'[6]

The Empress went to Nauheim, and consulted Dr Grotte who did not find any sign of heart disease from which Alexandra was convinced she was suffering. In 1919, when an inquest was held on the murder of the imperial family, Madeleine Zinotti, the maid who had spent her life in the Empress's service, talked about her mistress's health:

I spent nearly my entire life with the Empress. I knew her well and had much affection for her. It seems to me that the Empress was ill during the last years of her life. It seems to me that she was suffering from hysteria. . . . What was the cause of the

The Tsarina resting in her boudoir, 1908. She frequently remained there for days at a time.

Empress' hysterical condition I do not know. Perhaps she was suffering from a woman's disease. . . . Dr Grotte found symptoms of a nervous ailment for which he prescribed quite a different treatment from the one which she had been following. Later Dr Fisher found the same thing. He presented to the Emperor a secret report. . . . Fisher . . . insisted on treating – not her heart which he found in good condition – but her nervous system. In some way or other the Empress heard about this report by Fisher and he was instantly dismissed and replaced by Botkin who was, on her express desire, appointed her physician. . . . Observing her as I had the daily opportunity of doing, I was always surprised by one thing. When she found herself among congenial people she was always quite well, and never complained about her heart; but the moment anything displeased her . . . she immediately began to complain. Believing that her heart was affected she used to spend the greater part of the day lying on her sofa. . . .[7]

Alexandra on the balcony at Tsarskoe Selo.

In the autumn of 1912 the Empress forgot her own ailments, for Alexis nearly died. The family went to a hunting lodge in Poland where the Tsar shot big game. Shortly after their arrival Alexis jumped from a boat and fell, an oarlock grinding into his thigh near the groin. After a day or two in bed he seemed to recover and the family moved on to Spala near Warsaw. But the boy suddenly took a turn for the worse and the Empress wired Anna Vyrubova to come. When she arrived she found the family living in a large wooden palace so damp and dark that the electric lights had to stay on all day.

Two new doctors had been summoned from St Petersburg to join the two already there. The boy was suffering from a severe haemorrhage in the thigh and groin which had now spread to the abdomen. For some extraordinary reason the doctors did not believe in administering pain killers so the child was in agony. 'He hardly slept at all,' Nicholas later wrote to his mother, 'had not even the strength to cry, just moaned and kept repeating, "Oh Lord have mercy upon me."'[8]

Alexis.

For eleven days the boy moaned and cried for help, until members of the suite blocked their ears to keep out the pitiful sounds. Anna wrote that:

During the entire time, the Empress never undressed, never went to bed, rarely even laid down for an hour's rest. Hour after hour she sat beside the bed where the half-conscious child lay huddled on one side, his left leg drawn up so sharply that for nearly a year afterwards he could not straighten it out. His face was absolutely bloodless, drawn and seamed with suffering, while his almost expressionless eyes rolled back in his head. Once when the Emperor came into the room, seeing the boy in this agony, and hearing his faint screams of pain, the poor father's courage completely gave way and he rushed, weeping bitterly, to his study.[9]

No one thought the Tsarevich could live; not the doctors, not the parents, not even Alexis himself who asked his mother to build him a little monument in the woods. Count Fredericks received permission to start telegraphing medical bulletins to St Petersburg. Although there was no mention of the nature of the illness, special services were held in cathedrals and churches all over Russia. That night, when all hope was gone, the last sacrament was administered and a bulletin issued preparing the public for the boy's death.

At this point Alexandra asked Anna Vyrobuva to telegraph to Rasputin who was at Pokrovskoe, his home in Siberia, begging him to pray for the life of her son. Rasputin replied at once. 'God has seen your tears and heard your prayers. Do not grieve. The Little One will not die. Do not allow the doctors to bother him too much.' The telegram arrived in the middle of the night, and although by morning the bleeding still continued, Alexandra appeared for breakfast pale but smiling. 'During the night I received a telegram from Father Gregory,' she explained, 'and he has reassured me completely.'

At two o'clock that afternoon the haemorrhage stopped.

The rôle played by Rasputin at Spala was baffling. Since the nature of the Tsarevich's illness and Rasputin's interventions were still a secret, none of these incidents was discussed until after the war. When the facts eventually came to light most historians inclined toward the view that the *starets* possessed extraordinary hypnotic powers. Yet Spala seemed to throw a spanner into the works. Until this incident Rasputin had always appeared in person and prayed at the foot of the child's bed, which seemed to suggest some form of thought transference. But at Spala there was no Rasputin, only a telegram from Siberia. What sort of hypnosis was this?

There is another question that has no answer. If the Empress had complete faith in Rasputin, why, at Spala, did she not telegraph to him in the early days of the child's illness, rather than at the eleventh hour, when hope was abandoned and the last sacrament had been administered? Perhaps the most obvious explanation of Rasputin's 'powers' has been ignored. It is not unusual for a haemophiliac child to grow to manhood. Queen Victoria's son, Prince Leopold, who suffered from the disease, lived to the age of thirty-one; the two haemophiliac sons of Alexandra's aunt, Princess Beatrice, wife of Prince Henry of Battenberg, survived for over twenty years, while her sister, Princess Irene, married to Prince Henry of Prussia, had one haemophiliac son who lived until over the age of fifty, and another still alive in 1977. In all these cases the sufferers had severe haemorrhages which continued for hours and even days but eventually ceased of their own accord. This is a medically acknowledged pattern. No one knows why the bleeding stops, but if the child is to survive, stop it must. It is arguable, therefore, that the Tsarevich might have recovered from his many ordeals without the help of Rasputin – just as his cousins did. Furthermore, there were no eye-witnesses when Rasputin visited the sick-room, except the occasional presence of Anna Vyrubova, and so we have no reliable knowledge as to how often his help was sought, or how soon after his visits the bleeding stopped.

This is not to suggest that Rasputin was any ordinary, run-of-the-mill man. His picturesque language and powerful personality impressed the sophisticated as well as the naive. It was remarkable enough that an illiterate peasant could have made such an impression on eminent clergymen that they were eager to recommend him to the Empress. He built his reputation largely on prophecy, foretelling all sorts of happenings from marital upheavals and assassinations to defeat in war. Unfortunately no record was kept of the predictions that failed to materialize. Most human beings like to believe that a link with the supernatural is possible, and they tend to disregard the inaccuracies that upset their theories.

One of the Prime Minister's chief anxieties throughout 1912–13 was the irresponsible, happy-go-lucky attitude of the War Minister, General Sukhomlinov, who stood high in the sovereign's favour.

No more unlikely person to command the respect of Nicholas II and his deeply religious wife could possibly be imagined. Not only was Sukhomlinov dishonest and unprincipled, but in 1908 he had run off with a married lady, Madame Ekaterina Boutovich – which had resulted in a scandalous divorce case. The following year, at the age of sixty-one, he married Ekaterina, and a few months later was nominated Minister of War. People whispered that he had bought the appointment by paying a large sum of money to Prince Andronnikov, a disreputable adventurer known to be a friend of Rasputin. Undoubtedly some influence was used, since it is inconceivable that Nicholas II would have selected Sukhomlinov of his own accord at this particular moment in his career.

Once chosen, the new War Minister succeeded in firmly establishing himself in the Tsar's good graces. The general had a fund of amusing stories; presented his reports briefly; and sensing the Tsar's unbounded admiration for the military, always praised the army and declared it 'fit as a fiddle and ready to fight'. The fact that Sukhomlinov did not hesitate to invent whatever he thought would please his Emperor made his task relatively easy. 'In spite of his mature age,' wrote Serge Sazonov, the Foreign Secretary, 'Sukhomlinov was ... eager for pleasure like a youth. ... It was very difficult to make him work, but to get him to tell the truth was well nigh impossible.'[10]

The General wore gold bracelets and was scented and pomaded. His pleasures, including his frivolous wife, were very expensive. Ekaterina insisted on spending her winters in the south of France where she entertained with abandon and was much admired for her fashionable dresses. However, Sukhomlinov was not worried about money for he had the enviable privilege of alloting new army contracts. Apart from this bonanza generous bonuses were paid for travel and Sukhomlinov frequently journeyed to Vladivostok and back, an 8,000-mile round trip. Once there, he rarely left the train, sitting snugly in his carriage, basking in the delightful thought that he had profited handsomely from doing his duty.

The annexation crisis was the first taste that European diplomacy had of 'the big lie', a technique that was to become increasingly popular as the century progressed. But Izvolsky did not stop here. Relieved of his post as Foreign Minister, he was sent as Ambassador to Paris, from where he was able to

Army officers cheering the Tsar after a review of troops outside Moscow.

organize a very effective cold war against Austria–Hungary, using Serbia as his lynch-pin. The technique was not new. For many years Russian diplomacy had promoted clandestine activities in support of its foreign policy.

Yet Izvolsky gave the game a fresh impetus by appealing to the younger generation of Serbs to work for 'a future reckoning'. As early as March 1909 he had managed to extract a promise from his Foreign Office that all Serbian nationalist propaganda would be financed by Russia; he therefore had no difficulty in finding left-wing students to devote themselves to his cause. The fact that Tsarist Russia was locking up its own left-wing students at home did not seem to cause the Russian Foreign Office the slightest embarrassment. Ever since the 1870s it had been accepted policy to encourage revolutionaries abroad and to suppress them at home. Indeed, for years the most conservative Panslavists had seen nothing odd in working hand-in-glove with foreign revolutionaries. Yet the game was growing dangerous, for the advance in twentieth-century communications made it impossible to keep the two groups apart. They were borrowing each other's techniques, provoking and nourishing each others' ambitions.

The key organization through which Russia worked in Belgrade was the *Narodna Obrana*, the para-military defence organization which had sprung into being over the annexation. Administered, oddly enough, by an Austrian Army officer who had fled from Vienna because of his revolutionary activities, the major soon turned the group into an agency for espionage and subversion throughout southern Austria. He encouraged them to organize cells, based on the Russian revolutionary system of groups of five, that would link the villages of Bosnia and Herzegovina; this, he explained, would enable the *Narodna Obrana* to 'prepare the people ideologically'. Two years later, in 1911, another and more violent secret society sprang up – The Black Hand – which was organized by Colonel Apis, soon to become head of the Serbian Intelligence Service; the watch-word was 'death', and, appropriately enough, in 1914 it successfully organized the assassination of the heir to the Austrian throne.

In this highly charged atmosphere the Tsar's first minister, Kokovtsov, lived in a state of permanent apprehension that General Sukhomlinov might make some foolhardy gesture that would involve Russia in war. His nervousness increased throughout 1912 as the year, like a shark with a host of pilot fish in tow, brought endless dangers in its wake. Most alarming was the news that the Foreign Secretary, Sazonov, encouraged by Izvolsky in Paris, had fathered the formation of a Balkan League in order, he said, to patch up the differences between Serbia and Bulgaria. Unfortunately the League was not pacific but belligerent, and celebrated its inauguration by attacking Turkey. The Austrians immediately recalled their fire-eating Chief of Staff, Field Marshal Franz Conrad von Hötzendorf, who promptly sent three divisions to the Austro–Serbian frontier to ensure that 'the little Allies' had made no territorial infringements.

The conflict nearly spread to the Great Powers, for when General Sukhomlinov heard the Austrian news he reacted impulsively, just as Kokovtsov had feared he would, and urged the Tsar – on what grounds no one knows – to order partial mobilization. None of the rest of Nicholas's ministers was informed of the decision until the Crown Council gathered. '... This partial mobilization refers exclusively to our Austrian frontier,' announced the Tsar, 'and we have no intention of taking any steps against Germany.' The Council was appalled by the very mention of the word 'mobilization'. 'Only the presence of the Tsar restrained us from giving vent to feelings which animated all of us,' wrote Kokovtsov. 'I stated quite frankly that the Minister of War and the two Commanders apparently did not perceive what dangers they were preparing for Russia. . . .'[11]

In the end the Tsar and Sukhomlinov changed their opinions and the mobilization order was cancelled. Afterwards Kokovtsov confronted the War Minister angrily and said: 'Don't you understand yet where you very nearly pushed Russia? Are you not ashamed to make such a game of the fate of the Tsar and your country?' Sukhomlinov defended himself by pointing out that he had taken the precaution of calling a meeting before sending the mobilization orders. Then he added, 'But we shall have a war anyway. . . . The Tsar and I believe in our army and know that a war would bring us nothing but good.'[11]

Despite the apprehensions of his colleagues the War Minister continued to take a belligerent line, declaring repeatedly that it was high time Russia 'stopped cringing' before the Germans. He was encouraged by the chauvinistic Grand Duke Nicholas Nicolaevich and his Montenegrin wife Anastasia, a sister-in-law of the King of Serbia. When the Balkan war began this lady talked excitedly about Serbia and Montenegro working together for 'a Greater Serbia'. She longed for her husband to grasp the leadership of the 'patriotic' forces in the country; and as a result he kept Panslav fever at a high pitch throughout the Balkan Wars by organizing 'Slavic banquets' which 'were arranged as a means of arousing general sympathy for the Balkan Slavs and of bringing pressure on the government for a more aggressive policy. . . .' Although the Balkan League had launched an aggressive war against Turkey, the banners referred to Russia as 'the Protectress of all the Slavs', while others read 'A Cross on Santa Sophia' and 'From Scutari to Montenegro'.

Nicholas II was becoming reconciled to the existence of the Duma. 'The Duma started too fast,' he confided to the historian, Sir Bernard Pares. 'Now it is slower, but better. And more lasting.' In the autumn of 1912 a fourth Duma was elected with much the same membership as the third. But there were a few changes. For one thing, the Empress had the immense satisfaction of learning that her pet aversion, Guchkov, had not been re-elected. Guchkov himself believed that his defeat had been organized by the police on instructions from the Empress – and was probably right. Nevertheless he continued to lead his party – the Octobrists – from outside the assembly, and remained as much in the public eye as ever.

On the deck of the Standart. *From the left : the Dowager Empress Marie Fedorovna, Nicholas, Olga, Tatiana, Marie and Anastasia. The dog, Jimmy, belonged to Anastasia.*

The most striking change in the new assembly was the advent of two new-comers who, in different ways, made history. Thirty-one-year-old Alex-ander Kerensky, a schoolmaster's son who hailed from Lenin's home town, Simbirsk, was a Labour member; or, in other words, a socialist but not a Marxist. That spring there had been an unpleasant incident at the Lena goldfield in Siberia when a drunken police guard ordered his men to fire on a group of perfectly orderly strikers. Two hundred were killed and Kerensky, as an energetic young lawyer, was asked to head a committee of inquiry. In June he was elected to the Duma, and since this gave him parliamentary immunity he travelled the length and breadth of the country holding meetings and doing 'strenuous political organizing and revolutionary work'.

The other newcomer was Roman Malinovsky, who posed as an enthusiastic Bolshevik representing Moscow's trade unions, but was, in fact, the *Okhrana*'s highest paid spy. Lenin was greatly taken with him and when Roman entered the Duma he was known as Lenin's protégé. His inflammatory speeches amazed his colleagues, who could not understand why he was not arrested. In 1914 he betrayed Joseph Stalin who was sent to Siberia; shortly after, Malinovsky abandoned his precarious life and slipped out of Russia into Poland. He made the mistake of returning in 1918 and was shot by the Bolsheviks.

Kerensky received every consideration in his investigation. 'I was not subject to the slightest pressure,' he wrote. 'No one could oust us from the courts, no one could lift a finger against us.' His report bitterly castigated the police and eventually caused the resignation of the Minister of the Interior.

LEFT *Kerensky, a socialist but not a Marxist, was bitterly opposed to extremist elements.*

Kerensky was elected to the fourth Duma at the end of 1912. He was a republican but he was also a passionate democrat; and as such he was deeply opposed to the handful of Marxist extremists – eight Mensheviks and six Bolsheviks – who had been elected at the same time. 'To me the two years in the Duma before the war were years of the most strenuous political, organizing and revolutionary work. The old, secretive, underground, conspirative methods of revolutionary activity had passed to the limbo of history. ...'[12]

Yet Lenin's supporters were so steeped in conspiracy that they would not have known how to operate without it. Throughout 1913 they slipped in and out of Poland to consult their leader. Lenin was disappointed that the Balkan conflagration had not spread. 'A war between Austria and Russia', he wrote to his friend Maxim Gorky in the spring of 1913, 'would be a very useful thing for the revolutionaries but it is not likely that Franz Joseph [the Austrian Emperor] or Nikolasha [the Tsar] will oblige.'[13]

Lenin's man in St Petersburg was Joseph Stalin. Stalin supervised the newspaper *Pravda*, launched in 1912 as the Bolshevik's official organ. He was Lenin's organizer *par excellence*, stealing money and inciting violence. In 1913, for the tercentenary celebrations, he printed a pamphlet on the shame of the three hundred years of Romanov rule.

But the year was not encouraging. Lenin's battles with the Mensheviks, who were no longer the minority but the majority, were bitter and tedious; and he was so poor that he found it hard to survive. That year he even contemplated giving up his work and emigrating to England to earn a living. 'There were terrible moments,' one of the Duma deputies records. 'What if the party cannot find any means? Then Ilyich will have to leave the movement, for he never gets his work into either bourgeois journals or newspapers.'[14]

Lenin clung on. The highlight of 1913, as far as he was concerned, was the news that his most trusted deputy, Malinovsky, had succeeded in wresting control of the St Petersburg Metal Workers Union from the Mensheviks. The news was relayed to Lenin on the day that Stalin was celebrating the first anniversary of *Pravda* – the *Pravda* which, says one of Lenin's biographers, 'somehow survived both censorship and police prosecution in an almost miraculous fashion, and reached a circulation of forty thousand'.

The fact becomes less miraculous when we examine Lenin's protégé, the brilliant Malinovsky. 'For the first time among our people in the Duma there is an outstanding worker leader', declared Lenin enthusiastically. But the truth was that Malinovsky was a double agent working for the *Okhrana*. Lenin wrote many of Malinovsky's speeches, but the police always vetted them first and prided themselves on knowing every Bolshevik plot. Malinovsky astounded his fellow deputies by openly calling for the overthrow of the Tsar. Although no one knew the reason, because of him *Pravda* was allowed to function untouched.

Malinovsky was not alone. With varying skills, thousands of Russians were playing the same double game. How far the pre-war revolutionaries corrupted the police, or the police the revolutionaries, no one will ever know.

Early in the morning of 6 March 1913, a salute of thirty-one guns from the Fortress of St Peter and St Paul marked the opening of the ceremonies commemorating the Romanov tercentenary. Troops in red, green and blue uniforms, some with helmets and breast plates, had taken their places on the route through the Morskaya and the Nevsky Prospect where the Tsar and his family would drive on their way to Kazan cathedral. There was very little enthusiasm. It was raining hard and the crowds were thin. The bunting on the lamp-posts and the flags on the key buildings hung disconsolate in the downpour. Even the standards of the famous regiments – Household Cavalry, Lancers, *Chevaux Légers*, Dragoons and Grenadiers – failed to arouse much interest.

Just before twelve the soldiers came to the salute, the bands struck up the Russian National Anthem and faces turned to the lofty archway of the General Staff building which spanned the entrance to the Morskaya. First came the trumpeters riding milk-white horses, then a company of scarlet-coated Cossacks of the Guard. 'Picked men those,' wrote the *Times* correspondent, 'superb riders and all reputed sharpshooters.' They carried their carbines unslung, the butt resting on the right thigh and the muzzle pointing upwards. They rode in double line and formed a screen for the imperial *cortège* across the entire breadth of the roadway. Immediately behind them came the open victoria drawn by two horses, in which sat the Tsar and the eight-year-old Tsarevich. This was followed by two state coaches, one carrying the Empress and her mother-in-law, the Dowager Empress Marie, and the other the Tsar's four young daughters.

The cathedral was filled with the highest dignitaries of the state. The huge interior glowed with ikons and candles while the Patriarch Antiochus, a fine old man in a mitre flashing with jewels, stood waiting to conduct the service. A hush fell over the assembly when the imperial family entered. The Empress Alexandra looked as remote and disdainful as ever. Behind her came the Tsarevich, painfully thin and drawn, in the arms of a Cossack of the Guards. A murmur broke over the crowd when they saw him. Everyone knew that he had been gravely ill at Spala six months earlier, but no one knew what was wrong with him. The foreign press had been speculating wildly. One paper said that the boy suffered from an incurable bone disease; another that he was born with too few layers of skin. The London *Daily Mail* advanced no theories but said that the child was being taken to Egypt for a treatment of mud baths.

Despite the public sympathy for the Tsarevich the capital greeted the imperial couple coldly. When they went to the opera Anna Vyrubova felt that 'there was little real enthusiasm, little real loyalty. . . . I saw a cloud over the whole celebration in Petrograd, and this impression, I am sure, was shared by the Empress.'[15] However the trip to Kostroma on the Volga where the first Romanov was born was a magnificent success. Some people waded waist deep into the water in order to catch a glimpse of the Tsar. Others kissed his shadow on the ground. 'Nobody, seeing those enthusiastic crowds,' mused the Tsar's sister, Olga, many years later, 'could have imagined that in less than four years Nicky's very name would be splattered with mud and hatred.'

Oddly enough, one of the few people who felt the hand of disaster on his shoulder was the German Kaiser. Throughout 1913 Wilhelm II was worried and subdued. He dropped his familiar stance as an avenging deity, sword in hand, and did everything in his power to smooth the troubles in the Balkans. His particular responsibility, of course, was Austria–Hungary and he

The Tsar and Tsarina during the Romanov tercentenary celebrations, 1913.
The public greeted them with little enthusiasm.

telegraphed regularly to the old Emperor begging for moderation and patience. Field Marshal Conrad von Hötzendorf, the powerful Chief of Staff, was not easy to control since he had been urging a preventative war against Serbia ever since 1909. He talked repeatedly about the necessity of invading Belgrade to put an end to the Russo–Serbian subversive societies now honeycombing southern Austria, and warned his government that if it failed to 'crush the little viper' the dissolution of the Habsburg Empire would take place before its eyes.

The Kaiser's surprisingly pacific attitude prompted the 1913 *British Annual Register* to choose him as the individual most responsible for preserving the peace of Europe. In St Petersburg the Holy Synod nominated a candidate of its own. 'That we escaped war last year,' wrote the Church newspaper, the *Kolokol*, 'is due to the influence of the Holy *startsy* who directs our foreign policy. . . .' Was there a touch of sarcasm in the statement? Perhaps; but Rasputin's warning, 'Fear, fear war,' was always in the Empress's mind and she constantly urged her husband to choose a path of conciliation.

The Grand Duchesses Olga and Tatiana, the Tsar's two elder daughters. LEFT *Olga (left) dressed in military uniform as Honorary Colonel of the Third Regiment of Elisabethgrad Hussars, and Tatiana as Honorary Colonel of the Eighth Vosnesensky Hussars.* OPPOSITE *Tatiana (*LEFT*) and Olga (*RIGHT*) in formal court dress.*

During the social season of 1913–14, from early December to the beginning of Lent, St Petersburg society expected the Empress to give a coming-out ball for her two eldest daughters, the blonde, blue-eyed, eighteen-year-old Olga, and the lively, dark-haired Tatiana, two years younger. However the Romanov tercentenary celebrations had so exhausted Alexandra that she felt unequal to any further effort. The great ladies of the capital, including the widowed Grand Duchess Vladimir who still ran the rival court, were indignant at being denied the pleasure of entertaining the Tsar's daughters, and criticized Alexandra's selfish, provincial outlook more fiercely than ever.

Perhaps the change of plan was caused by the chilly reception in St Petersburg; or perhaps to the Empress's long-standing contempt for the aristocracy which was even stronger now than when she had first come to Russia. She never allowed the Grand Duchesses to make friends with the daughters of the great Russian families, insisting that the 'dissolute milieu' in which the young ladies moved was bound to fill their minds with unwholesome ideas. Although all four of the little Grand Duchesses longed pathetically for the companionship of other girls, the Russian aristocracy

only saw them as remote and unapproachable figures who flitted across the official stage in white dresses and picture hats, as unreal as characters from a fairy story.

What made the situation even more poignant was the fact that the Tsar's daughters were not only pretty, but unaffected and charming as well. Fortunately they were not unhappy for long since they adored their parents and were so fond of each other that they loved doing things together, even writing joint letters which they signed by the first letter of each of their names – OTMA.

Their lives were lived inside the family circle which included their grandmother, the Dowager Empress, with whom they lunched every week, and their Aunt Olga who, according to Anna Vyrubova, arranged tea parties and tennis matches for her nieces, 'the guests, of course, being of their own choice'. The Empress frequently invited young Guards officers to the palace – usually those on duty in Tsarskoe Selo – and allowed the girls 'to have their little preferences for this or that handsome young officer with whom they danced, played tennis, walked or rode. These innocent young romances were, in fact, a source of amusement to their Majesties who enjoyed teasing the girls about any dashing officer who seemed to attract them.'[15]

When the Grand Duchesses went for a cruise on the *Standart* the Empress asked some of the ships' officers to lunch every day and frequently accepted return invitations to take tea in the mess. General Mossolov was amused by the innocent flirtations that took place. 'I do not, of course, use the word "flirtation" quite in the ordinary sense of the term,' he explained. 'The young officers could better be compared with the pages or squires of dames in the Middle Ages.'[16]

Perhaps the sisters' most striking characteristic was their complete obedience to their parents' will. No matter what was decided for them they never protested, never argued, never complained. The truth was that the Empress, by keeping her daughters in such a narrow protected world, safely isolated from all sophisticated or cynical or even unconventional ideas, was preventing her daughters from growing up. General Mossolov became aware of their immaturity aboard the *Standart*. 'As for the Grand Duchesses,' he wrote, 'even when the two eldest had grown up into real young women one might hear them talking like little girls of ten or twelve.'[16]

Nevertheless, in the spring of 1914 the Empress began to think of suitable husbands for her eldest daughter. Among those considered were the Prince of Wales who later became Edward VIII and ended by marrying Wallis Simpson in 1937, and Prince Carol of Romania, son and heir of the King, who in 1947 took as his third wife the famous courtesan Magda Lupesco. However in those pre-war days Prince Carol was eager to marry the Tsar of Russia's daughter and in June 1914 the imperial family took a trip from Yalta to Constanza, so that the young people could meet. The Grand Duchess Olga guessed what was happening and before her departure accosted Pierre Gilliard, her brother's tutor. 'Tell me the truth, monsieur. Do you know why

The Grand Duchesses Marie (right) and Anastasia, the two younger daughters.

we are going to Romania?' Gilliard replied tactfully that he thought it was for diplomatic reasons, but Olga knew better. She tossed her head and said fiercely: 'I don't want it to happen. Papa has promised not to make me and I don't want to leave Russia. I am a Russian and I mean to remain in Russia.'[17]

The Empress sympathized with Olga, although she once confided to Sazonov, the Russian Foreign Secretary, that it terrified her to think 'that the time was drawing near when I shall have to part with my daughters. I could desire nothing better than that they should remain in Russia after their marriage. But I have four daughters and this is impossible.' Alexandra went on to talk of 'the undreamed of happiness' God had given her in her marriage to the Tsar, and how she therefore felt it her duty 'to leave my daughters free to marry according to their inclination'. As a result Olga chatted amiably to Prince Carol but gave him no encouragement and parted from him as much a stranger as when she had arrived.

ABOVE Olga and Tatiana with their tutor Pierre Gilliard.

ABOVE Anastasia at her lessons.
OPPOSITE The boudoir in the Winter Palace.

No sooner had the imperial party returned by yacht to Peterhof than the young British admiral, Sir David Beatty, paid a visit to Russia, leading the First Battle Cruiser Squadron of the Royal Navy up the Baltic. The imperial family went aboard Beatty's flagship *Lion* for lunch. The Grand Duchesses were entertained by a group of 'middies' specially selected to look after them. 'Never have I seen happier faces than those of the young Grand Duchesses,' wrote the British Ambassador, Sir George Buchanan, many years later. 'When I think of them as I saw them that day, the tragic story of their deaths seems like some hideous nightmare.'

After Beatty's departure the family set forth on the *Standart* for their annual two-week cruise along the coast of Finland. Four days later, on 28 June, the Tsar received the news that the Archduke Franz Ferdinand, heir to the Austrian throne, and his wife, Sophie, had been shot dead at Sarajevo in Bosnia, then part of the Austro–Hungarian Empire. The assassin was a young Serb who lived in Bosnia, one of a group of seven youths, some of them students, who it was believed had been armed and trained in Belgrade.

Although this news was scarcely reassuring in view of the strained relations between Austria and Serbia, none of the sovereigns or presidents or prime ministers who stood at the helm of affairs believed that the outrage would lead to a World War. The Balkans were notorious as a hotbed of violence; if two Balkan wars in two years had failed to upset the peace of Europe, why should the Sarajevo murder prove an exception?

So the Tsar of Russia proceeded with his cruise, and the Emperor of Germany, who was also yachting, gave vent to furious anger but continued to race the *Meteor* at Kiel. The President of France, Monsieur Poincaré, attended to preparations for his state visit to St Petersburg, and the British Prime Minister, Mr Asquith, turned back wearily to the insoluble problems of Ireland.

The Empress Alexandra was too distraught to give much thought to the tragedy at Sarajevo. When her son, Alexis, boarded the *Standart* he had twisted his ankle jumping for the ladder leading to the deck. That night the joint began to swell and the following morning the pain was intense as internal bleeding began and the ankle stiffened. Gilliard, the tutor, found the Empress and Dr Botkin at the boy's bedside. Alexis was weeping and every now and then screamed with shooting pain.

This was bad enough, but more trouble was on its way. The day after the Sarajevo news a telegram arrived saying that Rasputin had been stabbed in the stomach in his village in Siberia and might not survive. His assailant was an hysterical woman who claimed to have been seduced by him, and who had followed him across Russia to kill him.. She accosted him in a back street in Pokrovskoe, and drove a knife deep into his intestines. 'I have killed the Antichrist,' she cried, then tried unsuccessfully to kill herself. Later she was sent to a lunatic asylum.

No one expected Rasputin to recover. He was rushed to a hospital, but the

OPPOSITE Chandelier from the House of Special Purpose in Ekaterinburg, where the imperial family were murdered.

wound had exposed his entrails and for two weeks he hovered between life and death. The Empress, frantic with worry at the thought of losing the man who kept her son alive, sent cables every night from the yacht. By the time the cruise was over Alexis was recovering and Gregory was out of danger. Nevertheless Rasputin was forced to stay in bed for two months which meant that he was unable to exert an influence over the momentous events about to take place.

President Poincaré's party steamed up the Baltic on the battleship *France* and docked at Peterhof. They were entertained at a spectacular military review at Krasnoe Selo and at a series of splendid banquets on land and sea. At the dinner given by the Grand Duke Nicholas Nicolaevich, Commander of the Imperial Guard and Commanding Officer of the St Petersburg Military Area, three long tables were set in half-open tents around a garden which was in full flower. The French Ambassador, Monsieur Paléologue, was one of the first to arrive and was given a boisterous welcome by the Grand Duke's wife, the Grand Duchess Anastasia, and her sister, the Grand Duchess Militsa. 'The two Montenegrins burst out talking at once,' he wrote.

Do you realize that we're passing through historic days, fateful days! . . . At the review tomorrow the bands will play nothing but the *Marche Lorraine* and *Sambre et Meuse*. I've had a telegram from my father today. He tells me we shall have a war before the end of the month. . . . What a hero my father is! . . . He's worthy of the Iliad! Just look at this little box I always take around with me. It's got some Lorraine soil in it, real Lorraine soil I picked up over the frontier when I was in France with my husband two years ago. . . .

At dinner I was on the left of the Grand Duchess Anastasia and the rhapsody continued, interspersed with prophecies: 'There's going to be a war. . . . There'll be nothing left of Austria. . . . You're going to get back Alsace and Lorraine. . . . Our armies will meet in Berlin. Germany will be destroyed. . . . Then, suddenly: 'I must restrain myself. The Emperor has his eyes on me.' Under the Tsar's stern gaze the Montenegrin sybil suddenly lapsed into silence.[18]

President Poincaré departed from Russian soil on the twenty-third, and that night Austria sent Serbia a formidable ultimatum demanding the dismemberment of all anti-Austrian societies, a cessation of hostile propaganda and the right of Austrian officials to take part in the search for members of the conspiracy which had provoked the assassination.

Today, when most of the facts are known, the ultimatum does not seem excessive. We know that the instigator of the outrage was Colonel Apis, the head of the Serbian Intelligence Service and chief of the secret society, The Black Hand. Later it was revealed that Apis had worked hand-in-glove with the Russian military attaché in Belgrade, who had encouraged the murder plot.

Austria was fully aware of Serbia's intrigues with Russia, and deeply stung by Belgrade's openly-proclaimed ambition to rob her of the provinces she had held for generations. 'For Austria to sit with folded arms,' wrote the

Drawing of Rasputin recovering in hospital after the attempt on his life.

что завтре? ты наш
руководитель боже
сколько въ жизни
путей тернистыхъ

eminent British historian, G. P. Gooch, 'and wait until her enemies felt strong enough to carry out their programme of dismemberment was to proclaim her impotence and invite disaster; and the murder of the heir to the throne by Yugoslav assassins appeared to demand some striking vindication of the authority of the state.'[19]

Austria, therefore, was determined to go ahead at any cost. What would Russia do? The Tsar remained at Krasnoe Selo for another two days watching the summer review of Russian troops. On the night of the twenty-fourth he attended a banquet and a theatrical performance at which the Grand Duke Nicholas made inflammatory speeches provoking a great demonstration for war. On the Grand Duke's orders the St Petersburg military cadets were promoted to the positions of regular officers in the army, instead of later in the year as was customary. Many of them openly expressed their joy at 'starting something against Austria'. Even the capital had caught the fever, for the streets resounded to the clatter of horses' hoofs as the Imperial Guard returned, a month early, to their barracks. When Ambassador Paléologue went to the railway station to say goodbye to Izvolsky, who was returning to Paris, they saw trains crowded with officers and soldiers. '*Cette fois, c'est la Guerre*,' they said.

When the Tsar summoned War Minister Sukhomlinov, Foreign Secretary Sazonov, and the Grand Duke Nicholas to his study at Tsarskoe Selo on the twenty-fifth, he refused to give the order for general mobilization. All three men used every argument for war that they could muster. Apart from 'not abandoning little Serbia', they talked about Russia's unique opportunity, secure in the alliance with France and Britain, to establish a hegemony in the Balkans. But the Tsar would only agree to move part of the way. In place of mobilization he authorized the military to make secret preparations under the regulation known as *The Period Preparatory to War*.

On the twenty-sixth, when the British Ambassador in Paris was informed of the threatening tone of the Russian press, he wrote in his diary: '... Russia comes forward as the protectress of Serbia; by what title except that she is, by right, protectress of the Slavs. What rubbish! And she will expect, if she adheres to the present attitude, France and Britain to support her in arms....'[20]

Russia's self-appointed role as protectress of the Slavs was of fairly recent origin; a pretentious and foolish idea that had been launched by the Panslav organizations to further Russian expansion in the Balkans. It had no historical roots, since Russia had never entered into any treaty obligations with Serbia. Furthermore, she had no quarrel with Germany with whom she had been at peace since the days of Frederick the Great, 150 years earlier.

All this time the Empress was doing her best to persuade Nicholas not to capitulate to the belligerent attitude of his ministers and generals. According to Pierre Gilliard she sent Rasputin heartbreaking cables at his hospital at Tioumen in Siberia. One of them said: 'We are horrified at the prospect of war. Do you think it is possible? Pray for us. Help us with your counsels.'[21]

Rasputin responded by telegraphing directly to the Tsar. 'Let Papa not plan war, for with war will come the end of Russia and yourselves and you will lose to the last man.'[22]

Anna Vyrubova tells us that the Emperor was 'plainly irritated' by the message, which he crumpled and tossed to one side. The truth was that Nicholas was in two minds about war. Although he was frightened of defeat he dramatized the army and could think of nothing more glorious than leading his troops to victory. Furthermore, Russia was again in the grip of industrial unrest and war might draw the country together. Firebrands like Alexander Kerensky had organized a network of socialist clubs all over Russia which stirred up trouble, and at that very moment over a million and a half men were on strike. In the Baku area oil workers had clashed with the police; and in St Petersburg gangs were smashing windows and erecting barricades. 'In one short talk that I had with the Emperor,' wrote Anna, 'he seemed to find a certain comfort in the thought that war always strengthened national feeling . . . and Russia would emerge . . . stronger than ever.'[23]

These impulses were only momentary, and Nicholas continued to teeter backwards and forwards, uncertain of the right course to follow. Meanwhile the Russian High Command was cancelling leave, moving troops, shoeing horses, rounding up spies, organizing food supplies, and doing the hundreds of things listed as permissible in the *The Period Preparatory to War*. Needless to say the Russian moves were causing great excitement in the German frontier villages.

Against this background of feverish activity the Serbs replied to the Austrian ultimatum. The answer was delivered on the evening of 25 July in a long and brilliantly clever diplomatic document. At first glance it appeared conciliatory but on closer examination the concessions were so guarded that they gave no real guarantee for the future. On the twenty-eighth the Dual Monarchy broke off diplomatic relations, and on the twenty-ninth bombarded Belgrade from Austrian territory across the Danube.

With reports of Russian troop movements pouring into Berlin, the Kaiser was so alarmed that on the night of the twenty-eighth he sent a personal telegram to the Tsar reminding him 'of the hearty and tender friendship that binds us both', of the 'dastardly crime' at Sarajevo against 'all Sovereigns', and assuring Nicholas that he was doing his utmost to induce the Austrians to arrive at a satisfactory understanding with Russia.

Strangely enough, the Kaiser's telegram crossed an urgent appeal from the Tsar – two cries for help passing each other in the dark –

. . . an ignoble war has been declared on a weak country. The indignation in Russia fully shared by me is enormous. I see that very soon I shall be overwhelmed by the pressure brought upon me and be forced to take extreme measures which will lead to war. . . . I beg you in the name of our old friendship to do what you can to stop your allies from going too far. Nicky.[24]

The Tsar's telegram was dispatched at two in the morning of the twenty-ninth, but nine hours later War Minister Sukhomlinov and Foreign Secretary Sazonov implored Nicholas to order general mobilization without further delay; the Emperor weakly gave in. The mobilization order required the signatures of three specified ministers and one of them could not be found. General Dobrorolski whose task it was to dispatch the historic telegram did not reach the Central Telegraph office until that evening. No sooner had he arrived than a captain of the General Staff came panting after him: the Tsar had changed his mind and the telegram was not to be sent. Instead an order would be drawn up for partial mobilization.

The reason for the change was that another telegram had arrived from the Kaiser, repeating the possibility of a direct understanding between Vienna and St Petersburg. It went on to say: 'Military measures on the part of Russia which would be looked upon by Austria as threatening would precipitate a calamity we both wish to avoid. . . .'

Much to the disapproval of the High Command the Tsar insisted on changing the mobilization order from 'general' to 'partial'. He then cabled the Kaiser that the 'partial' had 'come into force for reasons of defence.' 'I hope with all my heart that these measures won't in any way interfere with your part as mediator.' When Wilhelm II read this message he wrote indignantly: 'And these measures are for defence against Austria which is in no way attacking him!!! . . . It is only a manoeuvre to increase the start they have already got. My work is at an end.'[24]

The Kaiser's generals were eager to get the war under way, and in Russia similar pressures were being exerted, since all generals everywhere were afraid of being left at the starting post. Sukhomlinov's assistant, General Yanushkevich, who had been chosen for his servility rather than his competence, telephoned the Tsar on the morning of the thirtieth and implored him to issue the general mobilization order. Nicholas, however, threatened to break off the conversation, but finally agreed to see the Foreign Secretary, Sazonov, at three o'clock.

The generals begged Sazonov to use every argument he could conjure up – political and military – to persuade the Tsar to change his mind. If he were successful he was to telephone the Chief of Staff so that the latter could convert the partial mobilization into the general mobilization order. 'After this,' said Yanushkevich, 'I will retire from sight, smash the telephone and generally take all measures so that I cannot be found to give any contrary orders for a new postponement of the general mobilization.'

Sazonov found the Tsar pale and nervous. 'Think of the responsibility you are advising me to take,' he said. 'Think of the thousands and thousands of men who will be sent to their deaths.'

'The Tsar sat silently staring into space and could not bring himself to speak the decisive word. After an hour General Tatishev said: "Yes, it is hard to decide." In a burst of irritability the Tsar said: "I will decide", and immediately gave the order for general mobilization. Sazonov hurried to the telephone, notified General Yanushkevich and said: "Now you can smash the telephone. Give your orders, General, and then – disappear for the rest of the day.'"[25]

Apparently Nicholas did not dare to tell Alexandra what he had done. Knowing how strongly she felt that war would spell the end of the dynasty, he sat through dinner that night allowing her to think that only a partial mobilization order had gone through.

When Anna Vyrubova was in the capital the next day she saw the mobilization notices being pasted on the buildings, while the men cheered and waved their arms, the women wept and the children whooped with excitement.

I went to my evening duties with the Empress, [wrote Anna] only to find that she had remained in absolute ignorance as to what was taking place. Mobilization! It was not true, she exclaimed. Certainly armies were moving but only on the Austrian frontier. She hurried from the room and I heard her enter the Emperor's study. For half an hour the sound of their excited voices reached my ears. Returning, the Empress dropped on her couch as if overcome by desperate tidings. 'War!' she murmured breathlessly. 'And I knew nothing of it. This is the end of everything.'

I could say nothing. I understood as little as she the incomprehensible silence of the Emperor at such an hour, and as always, whatever hurt her hurt me. We sat in silence until eleven when, as usual, the Emperor came in to tea, but he was distraught and gloomy and the tea hour also passed in almost complete silence. . . . The extreme depression of the Empress continued unrelieved. Up to the last moment she hoped against hope, and when the German formal declaration of war was given she gave way to a perfect passion of weeping, repeating to me through her tears: 'This is the end of everything.'[26]

The Empress was not alone in her despair. The Russian diplomat, Baron Rosen, described mobilization as an 'unmitigated folly and arrant imbecility'. 'If it was meant to be a deliberate provocation,' he wrote in his memoirs, 'it was an appalling crime, the responsibility for which these three men, Sazonov, Sukhomlinov and Yanushkevich must share with the equally guilty advisers of the German Emperor, who caused the Russian mobilization to be answered by an ultimatum and a declaration of war.'[27]

Count Witte, who was abroad, hurried back to St Petersburg when war broke out, crying that Russia's participation was a piece of madness and urging that she should withdraw at once. 'Why should Russia fight?' he railed to Ambassador Paléologue, who, of course, was outraged by the Count's sentiments.

No one here, no thinking man at least, cares a fig for these turbulent and vain Balkan folk who have nothing Slav about them and are only Turks christened by the wrong names. We ought to have let the Serbs suffer the chastisement they deserved. . . . Now let's talk about the . . . rewards it will bring us. . . . An increase in territory? Good Heavens! Isn't His Majesty's empire big enough already? . . . And even if we assume a complete victory, the Hohenzollerns and Habsburgs reduced to begging for peace . . . it means not only the end of German domination but the proclamation of republics throughout central Europe. That means the simultaneous end of Tsarism . . . we must liquidate this stupid adventure as soon as possible.[28]

In 1914 Russia was inspired by patriotism and religious fervour.
The Tsar holds up an ikon to kneeling troops.

On 2 August the Tsar issued his own declaration of war and France followed suit on the same day. No one knows how many thousands of people gathered outside the Winter Palace. When Nicholas and Alexandra stepped on to the balcony many of them dropped to their knees. A moment later the vast crowd began to sing the imperial anthem; they sang it with all the fervour and all the faith, hope and despair that only war can inspire.

> God Save the Tsar,
> Mighty and powerful
> Let him reign for our glory
> For the confusion of our enemies
> The Orthodox Tsar
> God save the Tsar.

In that sublime moment Nicholas was for one fleeting moment truly God's anointed, beloved of his people.

5

War is Ruin

No country ever went to war so poorly equipped, so badly led, so foolishly optimistic, as Russia. The French contributed to the delusion by talking of 'the great Russian steamroller', with its potential of 15,000,000, which they hoped would share the impact of the initial German attack.

The Russian peasant–soldiers were too ignorant to be intimidated by an enemy they had not yet met. 'The Germans only know how to make sausages,' they quipped. 'All we have to do to chase them away is to throw our caps in the air.' Although the educated classes were not so naive as this, they had their own form of delusion also rooted in over-confidence. War Minister Sukhomlinov had been boasting for months that the Russian army could take on the Germans single-handed, while Kokovtsov concluded sadly that the Tsar and most of his ministers seemed to be under the impression that aggressiveness would guarantee victory.

No doubt it was this cheerful outlook, combined with the prospect of escaping from the boring routine of everyday life, that united the nation. A month before the outbreak of war a political stoppage had closed down a factory of 150,000 workers, bringing the total number of men on strike throughout the country to one and a half million. 'The German Ambassador had sent a coded cable to Berlin,' wrote Alexander Kerensky, 'that Russia was in the throes of internal disturbances and so unable to fight. ... But behold, war was declared; and all at once not a trace was left of the revolutionary movement. The workmen of St Petersburg returned to their factories. ... The mobilization proceeded in the most exemplary manner and was completed in scheduled time. ...'[1]

Mobs sacked the German Ambassador's Chancellery and hurled the bronze horses on the embassy roof to the street far below. The Tsar banned the sale of vodka and changed the name of the capital to Petrograd; and the Tsarina became the patroness of eighty-five hospitals stretching from Petrograd to Kharkov and Odessa.

The hospitals were needed. France and Britain had followed Russia into the war, and the German army was already pouring through Belgium *en route* for Paris. On 5 August the French Ambassador, Monsieur Paléologue, called on the Grand Duke Nicholas Nicolaevich, the newly appointed Commander-in-Chief of the Russian armies, who sat in an enormous study covered with maps. 'He came towards me with his quick firm strides. "God and Joan of Arc are with us", he exclaimed. "We shall win. ..."'

Paléologue told him that France would soon have to face twenty-five corps

The Tsar's daughters visiting him at General Headquarters, 1916.

of the enemy's best troops, and asked how soon Russia would be able to take the offensive. 'Perhaps', replied the Grand Duke, 'I shan't even wait until the concentration of all my corps is complete. As soon as I feel myself strong enough I shall attack. It will probably be the eighteenth of August.' When the Grand Duke bid his visitor farewell, he shook his hand crying, 'And now, into God's hands.'[2]

The Russians attacked in East Prussia using the First Army, consisting of 200,000 men under General Rennenkampf, and the Second Army, with 170,000 men under General Samsonov. Since each of these two armies was larger than the combined German forces, the object was to encircle and destroy the enemy, then to cross the Vistula and traverse the 150 miles to Berlin.

What happened was very different. The two Russian generals, Rennenkampf and Samsonov, had won their reputations as cavalry leaders in the Russo–Japanese War of 1905, and knew nothing about modern warfare. Indeed, when the swashbuckling Rennenkampf marched into East Prussia he ordered his cavalry to attack the German artillery posts. The result, of course, was the massacre of his best officers. He then moved up his own artillery and on August 20 achieved a minor success. But instead of pursuing the retreating columns, Rennenkampf decided that the moment had come to consolidate and take a much needed rest.

Not entirely satisfied with developments on the Russian front, the German General Staff dispatched a new pair of generals to East Prussia: Hindenburg and Ludendorff, destined to go down in history as the most famous partnership of the war. Gambling heavily on Rennenkampf's lethargy, Hindenburg decided to throw his full weight against the Second Army.

At this moment Samsonov was struggling across the rough country north of the Polish border, through birch forests criss-crossed with streams and marshes, trying to cover twelve miles a day. Russian organization was not good at the best of times, and on this occasion almost non-existent. Many of the men marched five days without bread; communications were so inadequate that even corps commanders could not maintain contact; orders were often countermanded a few hours after being given. 'Men who had spent the night digging a trench facing south', wrote General Knox, a British officer attached to the Russian army, 'were towards daylight ordered to retire a short distance and to prepare at once another trench facing west.' 'The Russians', he concluded, 'were just big-hearted children who had thought out nothing and stumbled half-asleep into a wasp's nest.'[3]

The German attack began on 25 August and lasted four days. Surrounded on three sides, and subjected to a withering barrage of fire, Samsonov's army disintegrated. As the general retreated through the woods on the night of the twenty-ninth, accompanied by a handful of staff officers, he said that the disgrace of such a defeat was more than he could bear. 'The Emperor trusted me. How can I face him after such a disaster?' In the morning he rode away and his staff heard a shot. Although they never found the body, they felt that honour had been satisfied.

The Kaiser named the victory Tannenberg in revenge for a defeat suffered by the Teutonic Knights at the hands of the Slavs in 1410. General Hindenburg then turned his attention to Rennenkampf whose supine attitude had been largely to blame for Samsonov's defeat. On 9 September he attacked the Russian First Army on both flanks and rolled up its left, taking a great many prisoners. Rennenkampf was not a man to fly in the face of fortune and promptly gave the order to evacuate East Prussia. This second victory was known as the Battle of the Masurian Lakes. Thus in three weeks the Hindenburg–Ludendorff axis had swept the area clear of invaders. 'With an army that averaged 150,000 men,' summarized General Knox, 'the Germans ... had inflicted losses of upwards of a quarter of a million men. They dealt a severe blow to Russian *morale* and deprived the Russian army of a vast quantity of necessary materials. ...'[4]

Nevertheless the Russian High Command could claim to have saved Paris. The Germans had panicked at the East Prussian invasion and transferred three corps from the western theatre. The troops did not arrive in time for the Battle of Tannenberg, nor was there time to return them to France for the Battle of the Marne. This futile violation of the famous Schlieffen Plan probably cost Germany the war. Conceived by the great von Moltke, hero of the Prussian victory of 1870, it was designed to place the German army on the Champs Elysées during the first month of the attack. Ironically, the plan was desecrated by the great man's nephew – another von Moltke – who suddenly had nightmarish visions of Russian hordes pouring into Berlin.

The Grand Duke Nicholas excused the Russian defeat on the grounds that his troops had hurried to the attack before the mobilization was complete. When the French military attaché offered condolences, the Commander-in-Chief replied in a debonair manner : 'We are happy to make such sacrifices for our allies.'

Meanwhile the Empress was working as a 'student nurse' in the hospital set up in the Catherine Palace in Tsarskoe Selo. She seemed to be a 'changed being' with 'every bodily ill and weakness forgotten', wrote Anna Vyrubova. Accompanied by Anna and her two eldest daughters, Olga and Tatiana, Alexandra reported at the hospital every morning punctually at nine. They went directly to the receiving wards where the men were brought in after first-aid treatment at the field hospitals.

They had travelled far and were usually disgustingly dirty as well as blood-stained and suffering. Our hands scrubbed in antispetic solutions, we began the work of washing, cleaning and bandaging maimed bodies, mangled faces, blinded eyes, all the indescribable mutilations of what is called civilized warfare. This we did under the orders of trained nurses. ...

As we became accustomed to the work and as both the Empress and Tatiana had extraordinary ability as nurses we were given more important work. ... I have seen the Empress of Russia in the operating room of a hospital holding ether cones, handling sterilized instruments, assisting in the most difficult operations, taking from the hands of the busy surgeons amputated legs and arms, removing bloody and even vermin-infected dressings enduring all the sights and smells and agonies of the most dreadful of all places, a military hospital in the midst of war. . . . I think I never saw her happier than on that day, at the end of our two months' intensive training, she marched at the head of a procession of nurses to receive the red cross and the diploma of a certified war nurse. [5]

After a month Olga was too unnerved to continue, and Anna transferred to executive work. But Alexandra and Tatiana were born nurses and never shrank from helping. Sometimes when a soldier was told that he had to undergo an operation which might prove fatal he would call out: 'Tsarina! Stand near me. Hold my hand that I may have courage.' Alexandra would put her arm under the soldier's head, comfort and talk to him while preparations for the operation were in progress, and with her own hands help with the anaesthetic.

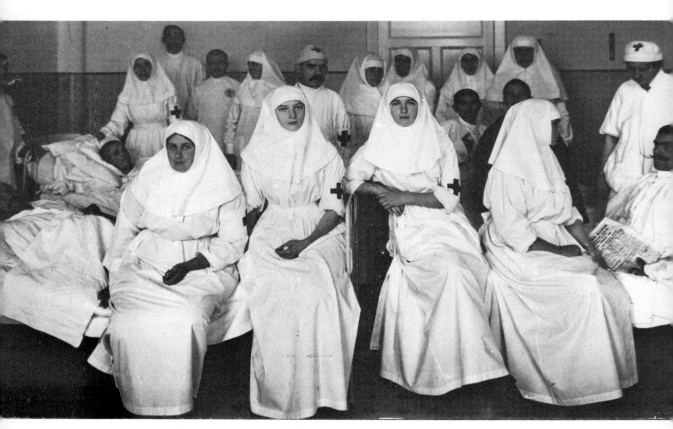

The Tsarina (right, in profile) with Olga and Tatiana, working as nurses at the military hospital at Tsarskoe Selo. The woman next to Tatiana may be Anna Vyrubova.

The Grand Duke Nicholas Nicolaevich visiting headquarters at Baranovichi, September 1914.

The Emperor was almost childishly happy at army headquarters. Here, as he put it, away from the 'intrigues' of the capital, surrounded by officers 'ready to fight and die for their country', he lived in the euphoria of optimism common to general staffs everywhere, and his spirits soared.

GHQ was known as *Stavka* after a Russian word meaning 'military camp of a chief'. It was situated off the main Moscow–Warsaw railway line, near the Polish junction of Baranovichi. Railway trucks had been extended into a forest of pine and birch, and in a large clearing guarded by three rows of sentries, the Grand Duke Nicholas and his officers lived in twelve trains drawn into a semi-circle.

The Commander-in-Chief, the Grand Duke Nicholas, was greatly admired by his men. Six foot six tall with blazing blue eyes, he was so imposing that many soldiers regarded him as a mystical figure. When the Tsar visited *Stavka* he was careful not to usurp the Commander's authority, while the Grand Duke managed to strike just the right balance between confidence and deference. The deference was not feigned, for the Grand Duke believed that Nicholas II was 'more than an ordinary man'.

When war broke out, Nicholas's first impulse had been to command his troops himself. He had been trained as a soldier, he loved the army, and he longed to share the tribulations of war. But his ministers argued that the prestige of a warrior–Tsar would not survive reverses; besides, who would run the country? So Nicholas acquiesced, and chafed and fretted. 'You have no idea how depressing it is to be away from the front,' he told Pierre Gilliard. 'It seems as if everything here saps energy and enfeebles resolution. . . . At the front there is only one thought – the determination to conquer. . . . I can never be in too much of a hurry to be with my troops.'[6]

Even in Tsarskoe Selo the Tsar could rejoice at good news. That autumn, soon after the Tannenberg debacle, the Russians had scored major successes in Galicia. They captured Lemberg, the capital of the province, routing four Austrian armies and taking 200,000 prisoners. As they were driving the army across the Carpathian mountains the French again made urgent representations, begging the Commander-in-Chief to ignore the Austrians and to engage the Germans directly.

Obligingly the Grand Duke broke off his pursuit, and mounted a new offensive in German Silesia which proved disastrous. For the first time the Russians began to complain of a shortage of shells. General Yanushkevich, the Chief of Staff, who had been so eager for war that he had cut the telephone wires to prevent the Tsar from countermanding the mobilization order, wrote panic-stricken letters to War Minister Sukhomlinov as early as December 1914.

Munitions are melting away. The Germans . . . say that we are at the end because we do not answer their fire; [and in another letter the same week] The shortage of officers is also keenly felt. Some of the regiments only have from seven to ten left. . . . Men have no boots, and their legs are frostbitten. They have no sheepskin or warm underwear, and are catching colds. The result is that in regiments that have lost their officers mass surrenders to the enemy have been developing, sometimes on the initiative of war-time officers. 'Why should we die of hunger and exposure without boots? The artillery keeps silent and we are shot down like partridges. One is better off in Germany. Let's go.'

Cossacks who succeeded in recapturing 500 prisoners were assaulted by them: 'Who asked you to do this, you sons-of-dogs? We don't want to suffer again from hunger and cold.'[7]

By the end of the year Russian casualties exceeded a million men – a quarter of those so far called to the colours. Proportionately, the officers suffered even more severely. The crack Preobrazhensky Guards Regiment lost forty-eight of its seventy officers, while the entire 18th Division had only forty officers left out of 370. The flower of the Russian aristocracy perished in the first four months of war.

In January 1915, the train on which Anna Vyrubova was travelling from Tsarskoe Selo went off the rails and capsized, breaking in two like an eggshell. Anna was wedged in the wreckage, a steel girder across her face, her legs crushed, her spine and skull injured, and her mouth so choked with blood she could not speak. One of the rescuers, a Cossack who served in the Emperor's guard, recognized her, but when the doctor gave her a cursory examination he said: 'Don't disturb her. She is dying.' The Cossack informed the Palace, and when Anna reached Tsarskoe Selo in a cattle truck fitted as an ambulance the Empress and the four Grand Duchesses were at the station to meet her. At the hospital a second doctor told the Empress to take leave of the injured woman, since she could not possibly live through the night.

Nevertheless, when Rasputin heard of the accident twenty-four hours later, she was still breathing. He rushed to the hospital and found the Emperor and Empress standing in her room. When he strode up to the bed Anna was unconscious, but he took her hand and called: 'Annushka! Annushka! Annushka!' The third time she opened her eyes, and saw the tall, gaunt figure bending over her. 'He looked at me fixedly and said in a calm voice: "She will live but she will always be a cripple."' A prediction, she continued, 'which was literally fulfilled, for to this day I can walk only slowly with a stick.'[8]

Rasputin staggered out of the room and collapsed in a spell of dizziness. When the Empress reached the palace she told her ladies-in-waiting that she had witnessed 'a miracle'. This incident alone utterly convinced her that Gregory Efimovich truly was a Man of God.

The Russian army refused to learn the lessons of East Prussia and Silesia; the Tsar continued to pin his hopes on a spring campaign that would result in massive victories and bring the war to an end before the year was out. By March 1915 the army had been renewed and once again numbered six million men, with nine million in reserve.

The Tsar with senior army officers during the war. Nicholas is seated in front of the flag-bearer, and the Grand Duke Nicholas Nicolaevich is striking a match on his left.

In April the Russians scored successes against the Austrians in Galicia. Nicholas II was at *Stavka* when news came that his troops had captured Przemysl, the enemy's strongest fortress, along with 120,000 prisoners and 200 guns. The Grand Duke ran into the Emperor's compartment and told him the good tidings with tears in his eyes. The Tsar attended a joyful Te Deum and presented the Grand Duke with a ceremonial sword studded with diamonds. Nicholas then toured the vanquished provinces and spent a night in Lemberg where he slept in the Emperor Franz Josef's bed. Meanwhile the Russian cavalry had crossed the Carpathians and descended on to the plain leading to Vienna. The Italians were so certain that Russia's victory was complete that they declared war on the Dual Empire.

Then the blow fell. While the Russians had been notching up their victories against the Austrians, the Hindenburg–Ludendorff axis had been

A public demonstration in the Nevsky Prospect, Petrograd, celebrating Przemysl, one of the few early Russian successes of the war.

massing men and materials in southern Poland, east of Warsaw. The object was a mammoth offensive that would knock Russia out of the war, enabling Germany to move her troops to the western front.

The onslaught began against a sector of the Russian Third Army commanded by General Radko Dmitriev; 1,500 guns fired 70,000 shells in the first four hours of the barrage. This gave war a totally new look, since no one except the Germans had ever envisaged such blistering artillery fire. Sir Bernard Pares, who was an eye-witness, wrote:

From a neighbouring height one could see an interrupted line of enemy fire from the heaviest guns for five miles to each side. The Russian artillery was practically silent. The elementary Russian trenches were completely wiped out and so, to all intents and purposes, was human life in that area. The Russian division stationed at this point was reduced ... from a normal 16,000 to 500. The enemy did not risk any advance until he had eliminated his opponent by metal.[9]

The Russians made mistakes as well. General Dmitriev had neglected to prepare a second line of defence, in the belief that he would be fighting Austrians who seldom moved up to the attack. As a result he made no fortified positions to which he could retire, and when the 3rd Caucasian Corps joined him as reinforcements, he was obliged to throw them into battle. They were quickly reduced from 40,000 to 8,000. Even so, they mounted a night bayonet attack at Sienawa and took 7,000 prisoners.

General Dmitriev was so shaken by his losses that he could only repeat again, and again, 'We have lost all our blood.' During this hiatus he failed to maintain proper communications with his neighbours – Evert of the Fourth Army and Brusilov of the Eighth – and they, too, were obliged to retire. This meant the surrender of the hard-won Carpathians. On 5 June came the loss of Przemysl, followed, seventeen days later, by Lemberg; by the end of July the whole of Galicia had passed into enemy hands. During the retreat Russian front line formations were reduced to mere skeletons. 'Recruits, young or old, drawn from anywhere,' wrote Pares, 'were hurried up into the line, often without a rifle, with instructions to wait for one till a neighbour was wounded. . . . Brusilov, who himself set about giving the recruits a training in the actual neighbourhood of the line, had now four to six of the old regular privates in a company of 250.'[10] 'In a year of war,' commented Brusilov, 'the regular army had vanished. It was replaced by an army of ignoramuses.'

By the time Hindenburg launched a new attack in the northwest of Poland, it took 'superhuman efforts to keep the men in the trenches'. The Russian officer who told this to General Knox went on to say that he had seen 1,600 newly arrived and unarmed recruits 'churned into gruel' by enemy fire.

Under these circumstances it was scarcely surprising that Russian soldiers were no longer eager for war. On 6 August, the day after Warsaw fell, General Polivanov reported from the War Ministry 'that an irreparable catastrophe' was pending. 'The army is no longer retreating but simply fleeing. Self confidence is completely undermined. The slightest rumour about the enemy, the appearance of an insignificant German detachment leads to panic and the flight of the whole army.'[11]

The general chaos was aggravated still further by the Grand Duke Nicholas's 'scorched earth' policy. As the army retreated it was ordered to drive the civilian population in front of it, leaving the advancing enemy a virtual desert. Although inspired by Kutuzov's tactics against Napoleon in 1812, there was very little comparison; the Germans had a superb railway system at their back and had no difficulty in supplying themselves with all their needs. The Russians, on the other hand, created destitution which soon came home to roost on their own doorstep. The report submitted to the Council of Ministers on 30 July 1915 referred to

... the immense stream of uprooted, desperate, suffering humanity that rolls along the road interfering with military traffic and completely disorganizing the rear of the army. They are accompanied by carts loaded with their belongings and by their domestic animals. It is impossible to provide food and shelter for this multitude. The death rate among the children has reached a terrible height. Unburied corpses are left along the roads ... and this flood of humanity spreads all over Russia, adds to the war-time hardships, creates a shortage of foodstuffs ... and accentuates discontent.[12]

In September Army Headquarters moved to Mogilev on the Upper Dnieper River and the Russian line was stabilized in the region of Pinsk, Baranovichi and Smorgony, where it remained fixed – except for the southern part – until the end of the war. 'The Russians had been defeated and forced back ... but the enemy had been able to thwart the enveloping movement on the Vilya'; and this meant that the army was still intact. Nevertheless the Germans had started a process of demoralization which eventually proved fatal. The total number of Russians killed, wounded and taken prisoner in the first ten months of the fighting came to a staggering sum of 3,800,000.

Nicholas and his retinue at Mogilev, 1916.

The only piece of cheering news for the Tsar, that spring of 1915, was the fact that Great Britain agreed to give the Russians Constantinople 'if the war was carried through by the Allies in unison to the end'. This was a fairly high-handed piece of diplomacy, but Nicholas II was enchanted, since he had always dreamt of being the conquering sovereign who entrusted the Golden Gates and Santa Sophia to the safe-keeping of the double-headed eagle.

Yet even this exciting prospect had paled by the time Mikhail Vladimirovich Rodzianko, the giant of a man who served as President of the Duma, visited headquarters in June 1915. 'The Emperor looked extremely pale and worried; his hands trembled,' he wrote. At that time the Russian army was in full retreat in Galicia and he had come to ask the Emperor to set up a Defence Council, on the lines of Britain's Ministry of Munitions, to supervise the production of ammunition. The extent of the Tsar's anxiety may be gauged by the fact that he not only assented, but two weeks later agreed to summon the Duma, which lived in a state of suspended animation, 'to hear the voice of the land of Russia'. Lastly, he finally dismissed Sukhomlinov, whom everybody blamed for the shortage of shells, and appointed General Polivanov in his place.

Meanwhile the Empress had moved on to the scene, a whirlwind of nervous energy despite the recurring ill health which once again confined her to a chaise longue half the day. She blazed with determination to save Tsar and Tsardom, not only for her husband and herself, but 'for Baby's sake'. Alexandra knew exactly how this could be accomplished. Ever since Rasputin had demonstrated his miraculous powers by 'resurrecting Anna' she had believed implicitly that he was 'a man of God'. She felt that she had a special and twofold mission: to save Russia, under Rasputin's guidance; and to preserve absolutism. In every letter to her husband she hammered the theme of the autocracy, and begged him to be more self-assertive. 'Forgive me . . . but you know you are too kind and gentle . . . be more decided and sure of yourself'; 'If only you could be more severe, my love . . . they must learn to tremble before you'; 'Remember you are the Emperor'; 'Be more autocratic, my very own sweetheart, and show your mind'; 'Never forget that you are and must remain an autocratic Emperor. . . . Russia, thank God, is not a constitutional country.'[13]

As for Rasputin, he revelled in the role created for him by the Empress, and gave her a steady stream of advice on everything from ministerial appointments to military strategy. He lived at 64 Gorokhovaya, in a working-class building smelling of cabbage and fish, where he received streams of petitioners well aware of his links with the palace. Several members of the secret police were always on duty outside his flat, and recorded all his comings and goings, not to mention the various ladies who spent the night with him, or who came running down the stairs weeping, saying that he had tried to dishonour them.

In April 1915 he had created a public scandal at the Yar, a notorious place of entertainment in Moscow. He got drunk and sat about with his fly buttons

The Tsarina and the Grand Duchesses,
a photograph taken in 1916.

undone. When asked by the management to adjust his clothes he replied loudly that the Emperor and 'the old girl' allowed him to appear that way in the palace. A British intelligence agent, Bruce Lockhart, was present and saw him being led away by the police, snarling like a wild animal.

General Dzhunkovsky, the assistant Minister of the Interior, reported the incident to the Tsar, who summoned Rasputin and questioned him. The *starets* admitted that he had been drunk but denied the other accusations and confessed sadly that he was 'a sinful man'. The Emperor did not show the report to the Empress for some time, but when she finally read it she was outraged, referring to it as 'that vile, filthy paper'. She did not rest until she had secured Dzunkovsky's dismissal.

The Empress saw Rasputin only at his best and flatly refused to believe that he was sexually depraved. She concentrated, instead, on the good side of his character. Although he could neither read nor write, he was not interested in money and, if it was thrust at him, usually gave it to the poor. When General Mossolov offered Rasputin a large bribe to cease interfering in state affairs, the *starets* only laughed at him. Rasputin was much too shrewd to allow himself to be used for the ulterior motives of others. It is quite possible that he was not nearly as much of a blackguard as historians like to claim. His aims sprang, as he himself put it, from the weaknesses of the flesh, and there was never a shred of evidence to prove that he was an enemy agent or 'run' by bankers. Undoubtedly he was genuinely devoted to the Empress, whom he extolled as a great ruler, and his initial opposition to the war stemmed from fear that revolution might follow in its wake just as it had done after the Russo–Japanese conflict. Later, his hatred of the holocaust was swollen by the terrible casualty lists.

Despite Rasputin's reputation as 'an evil man' he was not without a heart; he suffered for the bereaved and helped the poor and, with the assistance of the Empress, succeeded in improving the lot of the Jews. Lastly, although he cruelly deluded Nicholas and Alexandra he probably deluded himself as well, for there is no reason to doubt his tenacious belief in his own supernatural gifts. He talked a great deal about his 'will-power' as though it contained magical properties that would overcome all obstacles. Before he went to see the Tsar he spent hours preparing his 'spirit'; he knelt before ikons with charmed objects in his hand, begging God to allow his 'will' to prevail. As an untutored peasant who had succeeded in capturing the ear of the Emperor of Russia it is difficult to see how he could escape the conclusion that God was directing his steps.

Rasputin's worst quality was his vindictiveness, for he was a man who never forgave a slight. He hated the Grand Duke Nicholas Nicolaevich who, once upon a time, had received Gregory in his house, at the request of his wife Anastasia, and who had introduced him to court circles. Later, the Grand Duke had decided that Rasputin was a charlatan, and when the *starets* asked permission to visit the front to bless the troops Nicholas Nicolaevich had replied, 'Do come, and I'll hang you.'

Rasputin did not strike back until June 1915, when the Russian army was in full retreat. He had no trouble in prejudicing the Empress against 'Nikolasha', as she called him, because she had never forgiven him for the constitution of 1905. Now she passed on her misgivings to the Tsar at Headquarters.

12 June : Would to God N [Nikolasha] were another man and not turned against a man of God.

16 June : I have absolutely no faith in N – know him to be far from clever and having gone against a man of God his work won't be blessed or his advice good. . . . Russia will not be blessed if her Sovereign lets a man of God sent to help him be persecuted, I am sure. . . . You know N's hatred for Gregory is intense.

17 June : N's fault and Witte's that the Duma exists and it has caused you more worry than joy. Oh, I do not like N having anything to do with these . . . interior questions. . . . Nobody knows who is Emperor now. . . . It is as though N settles all. . . . It makes me utterly wretched.

25 June : I loathe your being at Headquarters . . . listening to N's advice which is not good and cannot be. . . . All are shocked that the ministers go with reports to him, as though he were now the Sovereign. Ah, my Nicky, things are not as they ought to be. . . .[14]

Nicholas II had a genuine admiration for his cousin, the Grand Duke; and Nicholas Nicolaevich was not only loyal to the Tsar, but believed him to be tinged with divinity. It therefore took the Empress six weeks to achieve her purpose, but she was helped by the fact that the Emperor was under pressure from his ministers to create a bridge between the civil and military authorities. In the middle of 1915 the Commander-in-Chief was virtually a dictator. The army authorities not only exercised absolute control over the field of operations, but over all the military institutions in the rear, from the Baltic to the Caucasus, from Finland to Vladivostok. Furthermore, no one bothered to work out the army's relation to the government. Indeed the prime minister and his cabinet were considered of so little importance that they were not even mentioned in the *Statute of Field Administration*. This, of course, meant that there was no authority to organize a civilian war effort; and that members of the Duma were rarely summoned and never used.

By August 1915, with the army still retreating, the Tsar decided to kill three birds with one stone: to satisfy his own dearest wish and lead the army himself; to please his wife by dismissing the Grand Duke; and to end the dichotomy between the civil and military authorities by combining the two in his own person.

When General Polivanov told the Council of Ministers of the Tsar's intention there was an uproar. Everyone knew about Rasputin's influence and it did not require much imagination to see that, with the Tsar at the front, the Empress would exercise greater authority than ever before. Since they knew that the Tsar was timid, and could only play the part of a figurehead, they feared that military decisions might come from officers with far less wisdom than the Grand Duke.

At a meeting at Tsarskoe Selo the Council begged Nicholas II to reconsider, pointing out the danger of leaving the government with no effective head and removing himself from the capital at such a critical time. He listened in silence, as stiff as a ramrod, an ikon in his hands, comforted by the thought that his wife at that very moment was praying God to maintain his resolve. He returned to the family drawing-room tired but triumphant, and told Alexandra that when the ministers had finished talking he had said: 'Gentlemen, in two days time I leave for *Stavka.*'

The distraught Council made one more attempt to prevent the Tsar from committing such a fatal error. Eight of the thirteen ministers wrote a joint letter of resignation. 'The Cabinet cannot perform its functions while it does not enjoy the confidence of the Sovereign.' But the Tsar merely summoned the recalcitrant signatories to headquarters and told them flatly they were not permitted to resign until he decided to release them.

The Empress was far more indignant, referring to them as 'fiends worse than the Duma' and saying they ought to be 'smacked'. Then she sat down and wrote to her husband an exuberant, exultant letter.

I cannot find words to express all I want to say – my heart is too full – You are proving yourself the Autocrat without which Russia cannot exist. . . . God anointed you at your Coronation. He placed you where you stand, and you have done your duty. . . . It is to be a glorious page in Russian history. . . . Our Friend's prayers arise day and night to Heaven. . . . Your sun is shining. . . . Sleep well my sunshine, Russia's Saviour.[15]

One momentous step followed another. Nicholas celebrated his new role as Commander-in-Chief by taking his eleven-year-old son, Alexis, to headquarters for an indefinite stay. The child was wildly excited and thrilled to be dressed in the uniform of a private soldier. His mother had never been parted from him and did her best to conceal her anxiety. During the first days of his absence, she bombarded Nicholas with instructions. 'See that Tiny doesn't tire himself on the stairs . . .'; 'Tiny loves digging . . . and forgets that he must be careful'; 'Take care of Baby's arm, don't let him run about on the train.'

Headquarters was now established at Mogilev, on the Dnieper River, where it had taken over the house of the provincial governor. Since the building was very crowded the Tsar ordered a cot put into his bedroom. 'It's very cosy sleeping side by side,' he wrote. '. . . He wakes up early in the morning between 7 and 8, sits up in bed and begins to talk quietly to me.'[16]

The Tsarevich had two doctors and two sailors to look after him, as well as his tutor, Pierre Gilliard. But his greatest joy was to escape from all of them. He liked to march up and down the garden path, his toy gun on his shoulder, singing loudly. When the foreign military attachés gathered before lunch for *zakouska* – hors d'oeuvres – he liked to tease and rag them. They made a great fuss over him and joined in all his games from hurling bread pellets across the table to playing drawing-room football, or to going out to the fountain and drenching each other with water.

The Tsar and Tsarevich leaving the garrison church at Stavka.

The Tsar was tremendously proud of his gay, good-looking little son and took him on trips to military reviews, hospitals, factories and shipyards. But the boy's health was always uppermost in his mind. In November, less than a month after arriving at headquarters, Alexis hurt his arm. 'He slept very restlessly, kept on sitting up in bed, groaning, calling for you and talking to me. Every few minutes he fell off to sleep again. . . . Thank God it is all over today except for paleness and a slight bleeding at the nose.'[16]

In December Nicholas took the boy to Galicia and a worse attack occurred. Alexis caught cold and began to sneeze, which started another nose-bleed, much heavier than usual. 'During the night the boy got worse,' wrote Gilliard. 'His temperature had gone up and he was getting weaker . . . we [started] back to GHQ but the boy's state was so alarming that it was decided to take him to Tsarskoe Selo. . . . The patient's strength was failing rapidly. We had to have the train stopped twice to change the [nose] plugs . . . and twice in the night he swooned away and I thought the end had come.'[17]

Anna Vyrubova was at the Empress's side when the Emperor arrived with his son.

His large blue eyes gazed at us with pathos unspeakable while the physicians kept up their ministrations exhausting every means known to science to stop the incessant bleeding. In despair the Empress sent for Rasputin. He came into the room, made the sign of the cross over the bed and looking intently at the almost moribund child said quietly to the kneeling parents: 'Don't be alarmed. Nothing will happen.' . . . That was all. The child fell asleep and the next day all was so well that the Emperor left for *Stavka*. Dr Derevenko and Professor Fedorov told me afterwards they did not even attempt to explain the cure.[18]

Rasputin was capable of all things. If he could save the Tsarevich, he could preserve the Tsardom and lead the Tsar to victory. 'Harken to Our Friend,' the Empress wrote to headquarters. '. . . it is not for nothing that God sent him to us – and we must pay more attention to what he has to say.'

The Empress's passionate belief in autocrat and autocracy had grown so strong since the challenge of 1905 that it now bordered on religious ecstasy; and with Rasputin as her counsellor, nothing presented a problem. As soon as the Tsar had assumed supreme command and taken up semi-permanent residence at headquarters, she applied her mind to ridding the government of the ministers who had signed their impertinent letter of resignation. Not only did they deserve punishment, but she was anxious to fill the vacant ministries with men blessed by Rasputin. She secured the first four dismissals in record time. Prince Shcherbatov, the Minister of the Interior, and Samarin, the Procurator of the Holy Synod, departed in October; Krivoshein, the Minister of Agriculture, and Kharitonov, the State Councillor, left in November and January.

Nicholas seldom demurred, and seldom made suggestions of his own. That autumn he wrote that he would have to part with 'Old Goremykin', his seventy-six-year-old Prime Minister, who was rapidly approaching his dotage. After protesting that 'he only lives to serve you', Alexandra accepted his decision and bounced back with the name of Boris Sturmer, a bureaucrat with an unsavoury reputation, who had served for a time at court as a Minister of Ceremonies, then as Governor of Yaroslav province. 'Lovey, I don't know,' she wrote, 'but ... Sturmer would do for a time. He very much values Gregory which is a great thing.' The French Ambassador reported to Paris on Sturmer. '... third-rate in intellect, mean spirit, low character, doubtful honesty, no expertise and no idea of State business.'[19]

The Duma was deeply insulted by the appointment, but worse was to come. In the autumn of 1916, the Tsar, at Alexandra's urgent request, appointed sixty-four-year-old Alexander Protopopov as Minister of the Interior. This little man with the restless, boot-button eyes was the son of a rich landowner in Simbirsk, the same town that had spawned Kerensky and Lenin. Protopopov was a member of the Duma – an Octobrist – and on several occasions had served as Vice-President of the assembly. He was charming and talkative, but so scatterbrained that his enemies explained his faults by saying that he was in an advanced stage of syphilis.

Since Protopopov was fascinated by mysticism he had become a member of Rasputin's outer circle; and the latter had pushed his name forward. 'God blesses Protopopov,' the Empress wrote. 'Our Friend says that you have done a very wise thing in naming him.' The Duma felt differently; Protopopov's colleagues were so indignant that they told him straight out he ought to resign. Whereas affability was enough for a Vice-President of the Duma, a great deal more was needed to direct a ministry. But Protopopov was full of confidence. An engraving of the head of Christ stood on an easel in his office, and he talked to it as a person. 'He helps me to do everything. Everything I do is by His advice,' he told Kerensky.

The appointments were calamitous, the dismissals sad. The Empress always referred to the Foreign Secretary as 'long-nosed Sazonov ... such a pancake'. She had long suspected him of liberal leanings, but when in the middle of 1916 he suggested an independent kingdom of Poland, she flew into a rage, arguing that 'Baby's future rights' were being challenged. Accompanied by Sturmer, she hurried to headquarters in a state of high excitement and secured his immediate dismissal.

Polivanov was liked and respected as a War Minister. He had displayed brilliant ability in transforming the beaten Russian army of 1915 into the well-trained, competent force of 1916. Unfortunately he discovered that Rasputin had been supplied by Prime Minister Sturmer with four War Office cars too fast for the police to follow him on his midnight outings. Polivanov protested and Alexandra immediately wrote to Nicholas: 'Get rid of Polivanov ... any honest man better than him. ... Lovey, don't dawdle, make up your mind, it's far too serious.' On 25 March, when she heard that he had been relieved of his office, she wrote: 'Oh, the relief! Now I shall sleep well.' General Knox felt differently. 'His dismissal was a disaster,' he wrote.

At least Polivanov had the satisfaction of seeing his new, streamlined army, commanded by General Brusilov, triumph against the Austrians in Galicia. The Russians inflicted heavy casualties and took 400,000 prisoners, which once again forced the Germans to pull units away from the western front – this time eighteen divisions from Verdun.

Yet the cost was heavy, and by the end of the summer the Russians had lost 1,200,000 men. The Empress and Rasputin began to interfere. 'Our Friend hopes we won't climb over the Carpathians and try to take them, as he repeats our losses will be too great ...', she wrote on 8 August. But the Tsar was persuaded by his Chief-of-Staff, Alexeiev, to continue the attack; and by 25 September Alexandra was beside herself with worry. '... Why repeat the madness of the Germans at Verdun? ... Our Generals don't count lives any more – hardened to losses – and that is sin.' Two days later Nicholas replied: 'My dear, Brusilov has, on receipt of my instructions, immediately given orders to stop.' Later Brusilov remarked acidly: 'An offensive without casualties may be staged only during manoeuvres.'

Rasputin and the 'German' Empress were seen as evil forces leading the weak Nicholas and his country to destruction.

'Sturmer and Protopopov both believe completely in our Friend's wonderful, God-sent wisdom,' the Empress wrote contentedly in 1916. She seemed quite oblivious to the criticism that was rising, like a high wind, outside the palace walls. The bewildering change of ministers, to which the Tsar tamely acquiesced, was undermining the last wisp of confidence in the government. During the sixteen months of the Empress's ascendancy, Russia had four different prime ministers, five ministers of the interior, four ministers of agriculture, three ministers of war and two ministers of foreign affairs. Members of the Duma referred sarcastically to 'ministerial leapfrog', while others found the 'rapidly changing succession of the "appointees of Rasputin" an amazing, extravagant and pitiful spectacle. . . .'

It was not only pitiful, but incompetent. With men like Sturmer and Protopopov controlling the key ministries, food, fuel and munitions began to run short. Sturmer's reputation was not enhanced when his private secretary, Manuilov – an intimate of Rasputin – was arrested for blackmailing a bank; nor when Sturmer himself tried and failed to draw 5,000,000 roubles from the Treasury without accounting for it.

The Tsar made up his mind that Sturmer would have to go. 'Prices are soaring and people are beginning to starve,' he wrote to his wife in November 1916. 'It is obvious where this situation may lead the country.' But when he wrote that he had decided to sack Protopopov as well, Alexandra became hysterical. 'I entreat you don't go and change Protopopov now, he will be all right, give him a chance to get the food supply into his hands. . . . Oh, Lovey, you can trust me. I may not be clever enough – but I have a strong feeling and that helps more than the brain often. Don't change anybody until we meet. I entreat you, let's speak it over quietly together. . . .' And the next day, 'Forgive me again writing but I am fighting for your reign and Baby's future. . . .'[20]

Alexandra took no chances and hurried to headquarters where she finally succeeded in imposing her will. Back in Tsarskoe Selo again, she wrote ecstatically of the 'great and beautiful' times that were coming, and before closing gave the usual advice. 'Be firm . . . Russia loves to feel the whip – it's their nature – tender love and then the iron hand to punish and guide. How I wish I could pour all my will into your veins. . . . Be Peter the Great, Ivan the Terrible, Emperor Paul – crush them all under you – now don't you laugh, naughty one.'[20]

This was not the only advice the Emperor received. At the front General Alexeiev warned Nicholas that according to the censors the soldiers wrote continuously about the Empress and Rasputin. He begged the Tsar to appoint a new ministry which would command the confidence of the Duma, but nothing came of his entreaty. The general obviously did not enlarge on the contents of the soldiers' letters, which often referred to the Empress as Rasputin's mistress, and Rasputin as a paid German agent. Indeed, even Anna Vyrubova was vilified as a member of the 'unholy Trinity', and accused of carrying messages between the Empress and 'enemy spies'. Every hardship, from the food shortage to the death roll, was attributed to their unscrupulous machinations. When General Knox toured the forward zone he was confronted by more than one bizarre example. A non-commissioned officer told him that he had seen with his own eyes 1,400 cattle being driven to the front so that they would fall into enemy hands when Vilna fell in September 1915. Even an artillery general, who should have known better, ended a discussion on the theft of magnetoes from motor cars by shrugging his shoulders and saying: 'What can we do? We have Germans everywhere. The Empress is a German.'

How did these wildly untrue stories gain such widespread acceptance? One can understand illiterate peasants being taken in by such fanciful tales, but why did the bureaucrats echo them as well? The truth is that Russians have always had a tendency to seek scapegoats for their misfortunes; it was easier to believe that the military reverses were the result of treachery rather than ineptitude, for the losses were truly staggering.

In the Great War ledger, [wrote Field Marshal von Hindenburg in his memoirs] the pages on which the Russian losses were written had been torn out. No one knows the figure. Five or eight millions? We, too, have no idea. All we know is that sometimes in our battles with the Russians we had to move the mounds of enemy corpses from before our trenches in order to get a clear field of fire against fresh assaulting waves. Imagination may try to reconstruct the figures of their losses, but an accurate calculation will remain forever a vain thing.

If the Russian bureaucracy was searching for a villain, Rasputin was an irresistible target. The *starets* had always been deeply opposed to the war. Although during the first months of the conflict he said: 'If we *must* fight, let us fight in earnest,' the reverses of 1915 horrified him and he complained bitterly that the villages were 'running out of blood'. He looked back at July 1914, when the outraged female had stabbed him, as the most unfortunate moment of his life. 'If only that hussy had not poked me with a knife,' he lamented, 'there would never have been any war at all.' Once he argued fiercely with the Tsar. 'You gave life to no one. Why should you take it away?' And in 1916 Prince Youssoupov quoted him as saying: 'This war ought not to continue, time it was ended, enough blood shed.'

Rasputin's opposition to the war was enough to start people whispering that he was working for the enemy, and he added fuel to the fire by frequenting the house of Manus, a rich banker, reputed to be Germany's chief agent in St Petersburg. The explanation was not at all complicated, as Manus's parties flowed with champagne and glittered with pretty women. Needless to say, Rasputin's friends and protégés fell under the same sinister cloud. Sturmer was suspect because of his German origin, while Protopopov was said to be seeking a separate peace. When the Grand Duke Alexander tried to track down the slanderous stories about the Empress his trail led him to the Duma, where he confronted several shamefaced deputies who said: 'If the young Tsarina is such a patriot why does she tolerate the presence of that

Alexis with some of his friends at Stavka. *His sailor-servant Nagorny is on the right.*

drunken beast, who is openly seen around the capital in the company of German spies and sympathizers?'

The Empress had very strong ideas about her unpopularity. 'Why do people hate me?' she wrote to her husband. 'Because they know that I have a strong will and when I am convinced of a thing being right (when besides being blessed by Gregory) do not change my mind and that they can't bear.'

177

Nevertheless she believed that the inarticulate masses were fond of her. 'Those who are good and simple and devoted to you honestly and purely love me, look at the simple people and the military.'[21]

When the Duma met in November the atmosphere was so explosive that many of the right-wing deputies attacked the government. The only change the Tsar had made was to sack Sturmer and to appoint a nonentity, Trepov, in his place; a month later he sacked Trepov and appointed a second nonentity, old Prince Golitsyn, who begged 'that this cup might pass from him'. Nicholas was adamant, however, since Golitsyn was deputy-chairman of one of the Empress's charities and Rasputin had blessed him.

Milyitin, the leader of the Cadets, delivered an attack that seemed to lend support to the stories of the Empress's treachery. He gave a long list of ministerial mistakes, ending each accusation with the words: 'Is this folly or is this treason?' The speech did not have much impact in the capital – most of the ruling class, particularly the aristocracy, knew that the Empress was anything but a traitor. Nevertheless they detested this cold, heartless woman who talked of preserving the autocracy while busily destroying the autocrat.

Many monarchists believed that if they could remove Rasputin the Empress's influence would collapse and the Tsar would reassert himself. On 2 December, fifty-year-old Vladimir Purishkevich, an extreme right-wing member of the Duma, made a slashing onslaught against the 'dark forces destroying the throne' – namely Rasputin, who need only flick a finger 'to raise the most abject citizen to high office'. He begged the Tsar's ministers to throw themselves at his feet to try to open the sovereign's eyes to the gathering storm. 'Revolution threatens,' he ended dramatically, 'and an obscure *moujik* shall govern Russia no longer!'

Listening in the gallery was twenty-nine-year-old Prince Felix Youssoupov, heir to one of the greatest fortunes in Russia and husband of the Tsar's niece, Irina. The Prince was tall and handsome and loved to play gipsy music on his guitar. He had studied at Oxford and caroused in most of the capitals of Europe. Lately he had been cultivating Rasputin in order to form his own estimate of him, and encouraged him to talk freely about the imperial family. Of Nicholas II Rasputin said: 'He is no Tsar–Emperor, just a child of God'; but he referred to Alexandra as 'a very wise ruler ... a second Catherine'.

For over a year Prince Youssoupov had toyed with the idea of murdering Rasputin in order to rid the court of his pernicious influence. After listening to Duma speeches, the Prince went to Purishkevich and told him what he had decided to do. The deputy threw in his lot with him and together they enlisted the help of the twenty-six-year-old Grand Duke Dimitri, a son of the Tsar's Uncle Paul. Youssoupov had to move carefully for, after the attack in the Duma, Rasputin sensed that his life was in danger and for a time refused to go out. The Prince spent three or four nights a week in his company, playing and singing. Then he invited him to his house, ostensibly to meet his wife, Irina. The princess was, in fact, on holiday in the Caucasus, but

Prince Felix Youssoupov, instigator of the plot to murder Rasputin.

Rasputin had always wanted to meet her and accepted eagerly.

The rendezvous was fixed for a midnight supper at the Youssoupov palace. A room in the cellar had just been redecorated as a party room and was attractively furnished with a Persian carpet and a white bearskin rug. In one corner stood an ebony cabinet with a valuable Italian crucifix of rock crystal and silver standing on top of it. On a low table in the middle of the room was a samovar, surrounded by plates of poisoned cakes. On the sideboard stood rows of bottles, flanking a bottle of poisoned Madeira.

Rasputin strode into the room, complimented the Prince on his taste, and sprawled out in an easy chair. During the first ten minutes he gulped down two glasses of poisoned Madeira and swallowed two poisoned cakes. But nothing happened. He bade Youssoupov play the guitar and sat back laughing and humming. Every now and then he asked why the Princess had not arrived. After an hour and a half he suggested going to the gipsies for a bit of fun. 'With God in mind,' he winked, 'but with mankind in the flesh.'

At this point Felix Youssoupov excused himself and dashed upstairs to ask his friends what he ought to do. Purishkevich told him firmly to persevere, and Dimitri Pavlovich handed him a revolver. When Youssoupov returned he led Rasputin to the cabinet to take a look at the crucifix. Rasputin gave it a cursory glance and said he preferred the cabinet. 'Gregory Efimovich, you had far better look at the crucifix and say a prayer,' said Youssoupov. Rasputin gave him a quizzical glance and turned towards the cross, whereupon Youssoupov, not very gallantly, shot him in the back. With a piercing cry Rasputin fell on to the white bearskin.

Dr Lazovert, who had mixed the ineffective poison, came into the room and pronounced Rasputin dead. His judgment was remarkably unreliable for a moment later, when Youssoupov was alone, the dead man opened his eyes and struggled to his feet. He lunged at Youssoupov's throat and tore an epaulette from his shoulder. By this time the Prince was convinced that he was dealing with the devil himself, and with Rasputin close after him ran up the stairs screaming: 'Purishkevich, fire, fire. He's alive, he's getting away.'

By this time Rasputin was crossing the snow-covered courtyard leading to the street. Purishkevich ran after him firing wildly. The first two bullets missed, but the third hit him in the shoulder and the fourth in the chest. He fell back, and both Youssoupov and Purishkevich, overcome by hysterics, kicked and battered the body. Then they wrapped it in a blue curtain and took it to the Neva where Purishkevich and the doctor pushed it through a hole in the ice.

The next morning soon after breakfast [wrote Anna Vyrubova] I was called on the telephone by one of the daughters of Rasputin, both of whom were being educated in Petrograd. In some anxiety the young girl told me that her father had gone out the night before in the Youssoupov motor car and had not returned. . . . When I returned to the palace I gave the message to the Empress who listened with a grave face. . . . A few minutes later there came a telephone call from Protopopov in Petrograd. . . . A patrolman standing near the entrance of the Youssoupov palace had been startled by the report of a pistol. Ringing the doorbell he was met by a Duma member named Purishkevich who appeared to be in an advanced state of intoxication . . . [Asked] whether there was any trouble at the house [he] said in a jocular tone that it was nothing, nothing at all, only they had just killed Rasputin. . . .[22]

Neither Protopopov nor the police believed the story, but the Empress ordered an immediate investigation. Then she dashed off a note to Nicholas telling him that Rasputin had vanished after a party at the Youssoupov palace where shots had been heard. 'I cannot and will not believe that he has been killed. God have mercy. Such utter anguish . . . come quickly. . . .'

Two days later Rasputin's frozen corpse was recovered from the Neva. Apparently the murderers had left one of his boots near the hole in the ice. His body was taken in secret to the chapel of the Veterans' Hospital near Tsarskoe Selo where an autopsy was performed. His lungs were full of water, showing that he was still alive when thrown into the river.

Two days later he was buried in a corner of the imperial park. An ikon signed by the Emperor and Empress and all five children was placed on his breast. Next to it was a letter from the Empress. 'My dear Martyr, Give me thy blessing that it may follow me always on the sad and dreary path I have yet to tread here on earth.'

With difficulty, Petrograd society restrained itself from celebrating Rasputin's death. Although the police amassed evidence against the murderers, public delight was so obvious that Nicholas II did not dare to punish them. Purishkevich was not arrested, and quickly departed for a tour of the front. The Grand Duke Dimitri was ordered to join the Russian army in Persia and Prince Youssoupov was banished to his estates in Central Asia. Ironically, these orders saved the lives of the two Romanovs from the violence of the revolution.

The aristocracy had been mistaken about the Empress, predicting that the shock of Rasputin's death would drive her into retirement. For two or three days she sat with a white, tear-stained face, staring into space with her beautiful blue–grey eyes. Then she suddenly pulled herself together and once again took command of the government. Although by this time the Emperor had returned to Tsarskoe Selo, the main telephone remained on her desk, which faced a portrait of Marie Antoinette. She now ruled with Protopopov, who tried to ape Rasputin and made a point of ringing her every morning at ten. She attended meetings with the Tsar's ministers whenever she could, and had a platform constructed off the Tsar's audience room where she could lie, concealed by curtains, and overhear her husband's conversations with diplomats.

Alexandra after Rasputin's death, January 1917.

Oddly enough, the Emperor seemed more distraught than his wife. He remained in Tsarskoe Selo for over two months, making his job as army commander more of a mockery than ever. He spent most of the day in the billiard room poring over military maps, and when Count Kokovtsov saw him he could not remember what day it was, and gave the impression of verging on a nervous breakdown.

When the Grand Duke Alexander met the sovereign, whom he had known since childhood, he felt that Nicholas was overwhelmed by his belief in fatalism, and had 'accepted his own ruin'. Undoubtedly the Emperor's state of mind was influenced by the prophecy which Rasputin had written just before his death. Simanovich, the latter's confidante, sent it to the Tsar after the murder, requesting him not to show it to the Empress.

If I am killed by common assassins, and especially by my brothers the Russian peasants, you, Tsar of Russia, have nothing to fear for your children. . . . But if you hear the sound of the bell which will tell you that Gregory had been killed, you must know this: if it was one of your relations who have wrought my death then no one of your family, that is to say, none of your children or relations will remain alive for more than two years. They will be killed by the Russian people. . . . I shall be killed. I am no longer among the living. . . .[23]

Never had morale sunk as low as in January 1917. The winter was bitterly cold, there was almost no fuel, and long lines were queueing for bread. General Brusilov's offensive had scored some successes, but had finally ground to a halt with a loss of a million men. Everywhere people talked of the coming revolution. There was nothing tangible, it was only an instinct, a premonition. Enthusiasm for the war had evaporated, leaving distress unchallenged which now was plainly visible in the pinched, sullen faces in the queue lines, in the unhappy emptiness of the villages bereft of able-bodied men.

A steady stream of distinguished men implored the Tsar to make changes in the government and to appoint a 'Ministry of Confidence' before it was too late, but he seemed incapable of action. Rodzianko, the Duma President, spoke to him in the bluntest language.

Chaos reigns everywhere. There is no Government, no system. . . . At every turn one is confronted with abuses and confusion. The nation realizes that you have banished all those in whom the Duma and the people trusted and replaced them by untrustworthy and incompetent men. . . . No wonder monstrous rumours are afloat of treason and incompetent men. . . . It is an open secret that the Empress issues orders without your knowledge . . . and that by her wish those whom she views with disfavour lose their jobs. . . . Your Majesty, do not compel the people to choose between you and the good of the country.

The Emperor pressed his head between his hands and said: 'Is it possible that for twenty-two years I have tried to act for the best and it has all been a mistake?'

'Yes, Your Majesty, for twenty-two years you have followed a wrong course.'

'In spite of these frank words,' wrote Rodzianko, 'the Emperor bade me a fond farewell, and manifested neither anger nor even displeasure.'[24]

A large section of opinion, however, felt that the Tsar had proved himself too ineffectual to be given another chance. That same January General Krymov, an emotional Corps Commander who eventually shot himself when the revolution came, addressed members of the Duma. He told them that everyone at the front felt a revolution was imminent since no one had any faith in the government. 'A *coup d'état* would be welcomed with joy,' he said, 'because the Emperor attaches more weight to his wife's pernicious influence than to all the honest words of warning.' The truth was that although the soldiers were fed up with the Government they were even more fed up with the war. 'The Russian peasant population never understood why it fought,' wrote General Knox. '... A higher type of human animal was required to persevere to victory through the monotony of disaster.'[25]

Everyone persisted in blaming the government, for they felt that only the government could change the mood of the people. General Alexeiev, the Chief of Staff, told Prince Lvov, Chairman of the Red Cross, that if the Empress visited headquarters again he would arrest her; and if the Tsar objected, he would be forced to abdicate. This type of action was advocated by the entourage surrounding the Grand Duchess Marie Pavlovna, the widow of the Tsar's Uncle Vladimir: for the Empress, a convent; for the Emperor, abdication in favour of his son.

Others persisted in trying to persuade the Emperor to act before it was too late. The British Ambassador, Sir George Buchanan, abandoned the language of diplomacy, and urged the Tsar to dismiss Protopopov and to appoint a new Prime Minister. 'Your Majesty has but one safe course ... to regain the confidence of the people.'

The Tsar drew himself up. 'Do you mean that I am to regain the confidence of *my* people, or that they are to regain *my* confidence?'

'Both, Sire,' replied the Ambassador smoothly. 'For without such mutual confidence Russia will never win this war.'[26]

The Grand Duke Alexander, 'Sandro' of the Tsar's bachelor days, was the most outspoken of all. He called on Alexandra, who lay in bed dressed in a white negligée embroidered with lace. Nicholas sat in a chair smoking. Sandro began by telling Alix that her interference in affairs of state was doing Nicky harm.

Then he went on to say that although he, Sandro, had always been opposed to parliamentary government, he had come to the conclusion that a ministry acceptable to the Duma was the only way to remove Nicky from the target area, and to direct the nation's wrath into new channels.

But Alix only sneered. 'All this talk of yours is ridiculous. Nicky is an autocrat. How could he share his divine right with a parliament?'

'You are very much mistaken, Alix. Your husband ceased to be an autocrat on 17 October 1905.'

'Remember, Alix,' Sandro continued, his voice rising. 'I remained silent for thirty months! For thirty months I never said as much as a word to you about the disgraceful goings-on in our government, better to say *your* government. I realize that you are willing to perish and that your husband feels the same way, but what about us? Must we all suffer for your blind stubbornness? . . .'

'I refuse to continue this dispute,' she said coldly.

'I got up, kissed her hand, received no kiss at all in reply, and left. I never saw Alix again.'[27]

The situation was not only tragic, but ironic. 'Protopopov', the French Ambassador had reported to Paris, 'is an outright monomaniac who will soon be placed in an asylum.' Yet this unbalanced little man, who could not concentrate his mind for more than a few seconds and who jumped from one subject to another like a yo-yo, was one of the chief reasons why the Emperor refused to heed his advisers. If he formed a 'Ministry of Confidence' Protopopov would have to go; and Rasputin had assured the Empress that Protopopov would lead her husband to glory.

So Nicholas II made his plans to spend a month at the front, leaving Protopopov in charge of the distribution of food and the maintenance of order, and in control of the police. For one brief moment the Tsar wavered. On 7 March he told his Prime Minister, poor old Prince Golitsyn, who had been begging him to make concessions, that he had decided to go to the Duma the next day and announce the formation of a responsible ministry. Within an hour Golitsyn was called back to the Palace – no doubt the Empress had intervened – and this time the Emperor told him that he had decided to leave for headquarters.

'How is that, Your Majesty?' asked Golitsyn, amazed. 'What about a responsible Ministry? You intended to go to the Duma tomorrow.'

'I have changed my mind. . . . I am leaving for headquarters tonight.'[28]

6

'God's Will'

As the imperial train slid across the grey, frozen Russian plains on Thursday, 8 March, carrying the Tsar to army headquarters, one of the Petrograd bread queues, composed mainly of women and boys, broke ranks and ransacked a baker's shop. The strict rationing was caused by the fact that, although the bakers had plenty of raw materials, they could not bake without fuel; and although the merchants had plenty of fuel, they could not distribute it without transport. Heavy snow had blocked the railway lines; 1,200 locomotive engines had frozen and burst, and 57,000 goods trains were stranded.

Over 70,000 men, most of them metal workers, were on strike in Vyborg, the working-class district of Petrograd. They flooded across the Neva bridges singing a sort of Russian *Marseillaise*. There were more food riots on the ninth, and on the tenth the Cossacks were called out to help the police maintain order. The Cossacks did not carry their whips, and fraternized with the crowds, calling out: 'We won't shoot.' The police had no such reservations. Their patrols paraded the streets and shot and wounded a hundred people.

Later a conservative deputy, Shulgin, wrote: 'The revolutionaries were not ready, but everything else was ready.' One of the revolutionaries admitted ruefully: 'The mass moved by itself.' 'Like the foolish Virgins,' a critic jeered, 'the revolutionaries were sleeping.' There was no order, no cohesion, no agreed purpose – not even any leaders. Just as statesmen and soldiers had been predicting, the elements of despair and defiance reacted on one another until suddenly a spontaneous combustion occurred.

On 11 March the whole of Petrograd seemed to be on the streets. Posters signed by General Habalov, the Military Governor, were pasted on all the public buildings warning the people that crowds were forbidden, and that if they gathered, the troops would fire. These notices had sprung up as a result of a telegram from the Minister of the Interior to the Tsar. Trembling in his boots, unable to exert authority, Protopopov had asked Nicholas II for instructions, referring only to food riots and neglecting to say that armed clashes were taking place. The Tsar replied directly to General Habalov: 'I command that the disorders in the capital shall be stopped tomorrow, as they are inadmissible at the heavy time of war with Germany and Austria. Nicholas.'

It was Sunday, so the crowds were huge, and no one took much notice of the posters. A few people carried red flags and some shouted: 'Down with the German woman!', but there was no violence. Three Guards regiments, the

OPPOSITE Cossacks demonstrating in the streets of Petrograd.
The placard reads 'Down with the monarchy'.
OVERLEAF Revolutionary crowds holding up the Petrograd traffic
'Liberty, Equality, Fraternity' is the legend on the banner
held aloft by the soldiers at the head of the procession.

Pavlovsky, the Preobrazhensky and the Volynsky, were ordered to disperse the concentrations. Two of the regiments fired into the crowd three or four times, but the Pavlovsky refused to obey, and when their colonel insisted, the soldiers shot him. The Preobrazhensky managed to disarm the regiment and moved it back to barracks.

Several left-wing agitators were holding a conference with Kerensky that night, and when they learned what had happened Yurenev, the leader of the Petrograd Bolsheviks, concluded that the revolt had failed. 'The reaction is gaining ground . . . it is clear that the working class and the soldiery must go different ways. . . .' The Tsar also believed that the disorders would subside. When Rodzianko sent him an urgent telegram reporting the disturbances and ending: 'May the blame not fall on the wearer of the Crown', Nicholas tossed it aside, saying: 'Some more rubbish from that fat Rodzianko.'[1]

The Tsar and Yurenev were wrong; on Monday the twelfth the Volynsky Regiment turned the revolt into a revolution. The evening before, the soldiers had argued far into the night about firing into the crowds, and the talk had resulted in mutiny. They killed their commanding officer and marched out of the barracks with only one lieutenant. All this happened at 6.30 in the morning. Two hours later the French ambassador happened to be looking out of his window when a military detachment came face to face with the mob.

At half past eight this morning, just as I was dressing, [he wrote] I heard a strange and prolonged din which seemed to come from the Alexander Bridge. I looked out; there was no one on the bridge which usually presented a busy scene. But almost immediately a disorderly mob carrying red flags appeared . . . on the right side of the Neva and a regiment came toward them on the opposite side. It looked as though there would be a violent collision, but on the contrary, the two bodies coalesced. The army was fraternizing with the revolution.[2]

That same morning General Knox called on General Manikovski at the Artillery Department and learned that both the Volynsky and the Preobrazhensky Regiments had mutinied.

An excited orderly rushed in: 'Your high Excellency'. They are forcing their way into the building. Shall we barricade the door?' But Manikovski had kept his nerve and said: 'No. Open all the doors. Why should we hinder them?' . . . . I went to the staircase and looked over the bannisters. Down on the ground floor, soldiers were taking the officers' swords, and a few hooligans were going through the pockets of coats left in the vestibule. I went down and found no NCO of the Preobrazhensky who was ordering his men to take only the swords and to steal nothing. . . . A party of soldiers was almost timidly breaking the glass of one of the arm-stands to take out the rifles – specimens of other nations, that were without ammunition and would be of no use to them. . . .[3]

All day long the mutineers poured through the streets, ransacking buildings and starting fires. The Law Courts had become a furnace, and soon other buildings hated for their occupants were in flames; the Ministry of the Interior, the Military Government building, the *Okhrana* headquarters, the arsenal on the Liteiny. 'Soldiers were dashing around the streets armed with guns and machine-guns,' wrote the Director of Police, Vasileyev. 'A roaring crowd invaded the quarters of the prison of preliminary confinement (before trial) and opened the cells; soon it was the same in all the prisons of the city. The police stations of the various wards were carried by the mob. Police who were not able to change into mufti were torn to pieces. The fire finished off the rest.'[4] Although only a handful of troops had remained with General Habalov he continued to fight, firing along the Nevsky Prospect with machine-guns.

That same morning, Monday the twelfth, the Cabinet had a meeting which proved to be its last. The ministers asked Protopopov to resign, and he agreed without demur. 'Now there's nothing left but to shoot myself,' he said sadly; but instead, he shuffled off and hid in a tailor's shop. The Grand Duke Michael, Nicholas's younger brother, telephoned army headquarters begging the Tsar yet again to appoint a Prime Minister who commanded popular support. General Alexeiev took the message and telephoned back to say that the Tsar was leaving for Tsarskoe Selo at once, and would make his decisions when he arrived in the morning. The Cabinet departed in despair, never to meet again.

The Duma was more robust. When Prime Minister Golitsyn sent them an order, signed by the Tsar before his departure, suspending the assembly, the deputies simply tossed it aside. Alexander Kerensky, with his pale face and his quick, firm decisions, stood out as a leader. He suggested summoning the members of all four Dumas in order to establish a basis of popular support, but his colleagues would not agree. He felt that it was vitally important to maintain control of the headlong rush of events, and had already taken it upon himself to send an invitation to the Volynsky Regiment to report to the Duma. Now someone burst into the room with the news that the Volynsky had accepted the offer, and was coming with its friends – the Preobrazhensky, the Litovsky, the Semyonovsky, the Ismailovsky, the Oranienbaum Machine-Gun Regiment, and many others – 25,000 troops in all.

'I must know!' exclaimed Kerensky. 'What can I tell them? Can I say that the Imperial Duma is with them; that it takes the responsibility on itself; that it stands at the head of the revolutionary movement?' No one would answer him, and then Rodzianko protested plaintively, 'I don't want to revolt.' 'Take the power,' advised the arch-conservative, Shulgin. 'The position is plain; if you don't, others will.'[5]

The soldiers arrived accompanied by thousands of cheering workers, and they all tried to flood the great hall of the Tauride Palace – the gift of Catherine the Great to her lover, Prince Potemkin. There was such a crush no one could move, and Rodzianko bellowed at them in his bull-like voice telling them that the Duma refused to be dissolved and had taken over the reins of government. That afternoon a temporary committee was established with Rodzianko as chairman.

Yet even then Kerensky continued to be the dominant figure. Shulgin, who later wrote a fascinating account of those turbulent days, said that Kerensky was the sort of man 'who could dance on a marsh', and this particular marsh had 'little hillocks on which he could find a footing'.

He seemed to grow every minute. The soldiers who streamed in consulted him and took his orders without question. And look! One of the first prisoners of the Revolution, Shcheglovitov, the ex-Minister of Justice, is brought in. He is in near danger of lynching, but Kerensky strides up to meet him, and says in his vibrant voice: 'Ivan Gregorevich, you are arrested. Your life is not in danger. The Imperial Duma does not shed blood.'[6] That one sentence saved the lives of thousands of people. The fact that there was someone in the Duma who could command them, made a deep impression, and the crowd stood about in the lobby 'as though in church'.

That same day a second organization established itself in the Tauride Palace, a Soviet of Soldiers and Workers' Deputies consisting of over 1,000 men and composed of one delegate of each company of revolutionary soldiers, and one deputy from every thousand workmen. This was Kerensky's handiwork.

From early morning, [he wrote] the rumour that the entire garrison had mutinied and that the troops were marching toward the Duma had spread all over town. . . . Naturally a question arose straightway as to how and by whom the soldiers and workmen were to be led; for until then their movement was completely unorganized, unco-ordinated and anarchical. 'A Soviet?' The memory of 1905 prompted this cry. . . . The Duma itself needed some representation of the rebel populace; without them it would have been impossible to reestablish order in the capital. For this reason the Soviet was formed very quickly . . . about three or four in the afternoon the organizers applied to me for suitable premises; I mentioned the matter to Rodzianko and the thing was done.[7]

The Tauride Palace had an immense hall and two long wings on either side, one of which was occupied by the Duma, and now the other was given to the Soviet. Thus, wrote Kerensky, 'two different Russias settled down side by side; the Russia of the ruling class who had lost (though they did not realize it yet) . . . and the Russia of Labour which was marching toward power without realizing it.'[7]

By Tuesday the thirteenth the revolutionaries had seized the Fortress of St Peter and St Paul, and the only spot left in the hands of General Habalov was the Winter Palace. The rebels gave him twenty minutes to move away or to face bombardment. Since there was no hope of reinforcements Habilov ordered his men to disperse and they faded into the landscape.

On that same day, the twelfth, the Empress telephoned her friend, Lili Dehn, the wife of one of the officers who served aboard the Imperial yacht, and asked her to come to Tsarskoe Selo to keep her company, and perhaps help with some of the children. Four days earlier, a few hours after the Tsar's departure, Olga and Alexis had come down with measles, followed by Anna Vyrubova. Now Tatiana had the disease and Marie was sickening for it. The

Kerensky in the grounds at Tsarskoe Selo after the Tsar's abdication.

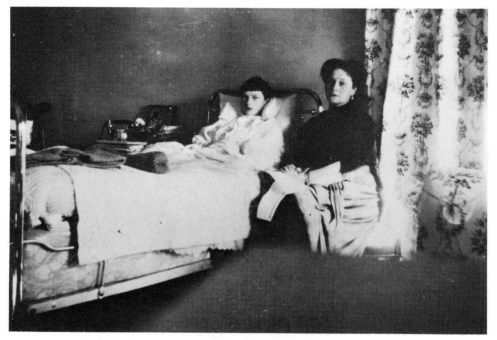

The Tsarina sitting by Tatiana's bed while her daughter recovered from measles.

Empress put on her Red Cross uniform and looked after all the invalids herself. They were very ill with high temperatures, and she went from one to another. 'I kept seeing her beside my bed dozing,' wrote Anna, 'now preparing a drink, now smoothing the cushions, now talking to the doctor.' Since Alexandra was on bad terms with most of the Romanov family, no one even rang her up to give her news.

Lili, who was both affable and stupid, arrived before lunch saying that although the general strike had made things inconvenient she had seen nothing alarming. It was not until Anna Vyrubova's father arrived in the afternoon that they heard a more realistic appraisal. 'Petrograd is in the hands of the mob,' he told them. 'They are commandeering all cars. They commandeered mine and I had to walk every step of the way.' Later the Empress was horrified to hear of the mutiny of the Guards regiments. 'I can't believe it,' she told Lili. 'I'll never believe in the possibility of revolution. ... I'm sure the trouble is confined to Petrograd alone.'[8]

That night a message arrived from Rodzianko, as chairman of the temporary committee of the Duma, saying that the Empress and her children were in danger and should leave Tsarskoe Selo at once. Count Benckendorff, the Court Marshal, did not show the message but telephoned Nicholas asking for instructions. The latter replied that he would arrive at Tsarskoe in eighteen hours' time, and said that the telegram should not be shown to his wife until the following day. When Alexandra finally read the message she shook her head, saying that she could not possibly move her sick children. In vain Rodzianko argued with Benckendorff that 'when a house is burning the invalids are the first to be taken out'.

The decision nearly proved fatal, for later that day Alexandra learned that a crowd of mutinous soldiers were on their way to Tsarskoe Selo: she was not told that the purpose was 'to seize the German woman and her son and bring them back to the capital'. Fortunately, the palace guard had been fortified and consisted of the most famous regiments in the land; two squadrons of Cossacks of the Emperor's Escort; two battalions of the picked Composite Regiment of the Imperial Guard; a company of the Railway Regiment and a battalion of *Garde Equipage*, the crack marine regiment whose sailors served aboard the imperial yacht. 'Oh Lili, what a blessing that we have here the most devoted troops. There is the *Garde Equipage*, they are all our personal friends.'

That night the Empress and her ladies sat together, nervously wondering when the attack would begin. Suddenly the Empress decided to go out and talk to the men herself. The Baroness Buxhoevden, one of the ladies-in-waiting, watched from an upstairs window. 'It was dark except for a faint light thrown up from the snow and reflected on the polished barrels of the rifles. The troops were lined up in battle order ... the first kneeling in the snow, the other standing behind their rifles in readiness for a sudden attack.'[9] With a black fur coat thrown over her white nurse's uniform, the Empress walked along the lines, her daughter Marie following, telling the men that they held the life of her son in their hands and that she trusted them completely. She did not seem to notice the surly replies and, according to Lili, came back to the palace 'apparently possessed by some inward exaltation'. 'They are all our friends', she kept repeating. 'They are all devoted to us.' She gave orders that the men should come into the kitchen in turns to warm themselves and drink tea. Alexandra stayed up most of the night for she expected her husband at six in the morning. At eight o'clock she learned that the imperial train had been stopped outside a station a hundred miles away.

The Tsar's train came to a halt at two o'clock in the morning when an officer boarded it to tell Nicholas's ADC that revolutionary soldiers with machine-guns and artillery were only a few miles up the track. Nicholas was awakened and after a brief discussion decided to go to Pskov, General Ruzsky's headquarters for the Northern Group of Armies. The imperial train did not reach Pskov until eight that evening and Nicholas was told that the entire garrison of Petrograd and Tsarskoe Selo had gone over to the revolutionaries, including the Cossack Escort and the *Garde Equipage*.

It was now the night of Wednesday the fourteenth; and the Tsar at long last decided to give the Duma what, for so many months, it had been begging. General Ruzsky wired Rodzianko that the Tsar offered a ministry acceptable to the Duma with a prime minister who would have full control of internal affairs. Rodzianko must have thought he was dreaming when he received this communication, for things had moved so far and so fast that the concession seemed hopelessly out of date.

His Majesty and yourself [he telegraphed to Ruszky] apparently are unable to realize what is happening in the capital. A terrible revolution has broken out. Hatred of the Empress has reached fever pitch. To prevent bloodshed I have been forced to arrest all the ministers. ... Don't send any more troops. I am hanging by a thread myself. Power is slipping from my hands. The measures you propose are too late. The time for them is gone. There is no return.[10]

That same morning the Soviet supported the Duma in appointing new ministers who would form a Duma Executive Committee until a constituent assembly, based on universal suffrage, was elected. The Soviet refused to sanction Rodzianko as Prime Minister, saying he was too conservative, so Prince Lvov, head of the *Zemstvo* Red Cross, was chosen. Miliukov, leader of the Cadets, became Foreign Minister, and Guchkov, leader of the Octobrists, War Minister. Kerensky emerged strongest of all, for he not only was Minister of Justice but Vice-President of the Soviet. Thus he constituted the only bridge between the two groups, now acting as two governments.

Everyone, even the monarchists, had come to the conclusion that Nicholas II must abdicate. The Empress had incurred too much ill-will because of her dependence on Rasputin, and the Tsar too much contempt because of his dependence on the Empress. Early on the fourteenth, several hours before Rodzianko received the Tsar's concessions, he telegraphed to General Alexeiev who agreed that abdication was the only solution. The general accepted the task of sounding out the soldiers commanding the various fronts. By the following morning he had received all the replies and forwarded them to Ruszky's headquarters.

Nicholas's train reached Pskov late that night; after breakfast the following morning General Ruszky brought the telegrams to Nicholas and laid them on the table. They were unanimous on the subject of abdication. Nicholas was stunned. He went quite white, rose from the table, walked to the other end of the carriage and stared out the window.

There was no way out. The army and the politicians had joined forces against his sovereignty. After a moment of terrible, almost suffocating silence, he turned and said: 'I have decided that I will give up the throne in favour of my son.' The general presented him with a document, prepared by General Alexeiev, and he signed. It was dated 15 March, 3 pm. As two representatives from the Duma, Shulgin and Guchkov, were on their way to Pskov to witness the signing and to carry the document back to the capital, the Tsar had to wait for several hours; and as he waited he thought about his son's future. He sent for Dr Federov, who was on the train, and asked him whether he thought Alexis would ever outgrow his illness. 'Science teaches us, Sire,' the doctor replied, 'that it is an incurable disease. Yet those who are afflicted with it sometimes reach an advanced old age. Still Alexis

Nicolaevich is at the mercy of an accident.'[11] Discussing it further, Federov pointed out gently that once Nicolas was off the throne the ex-sovereign and his wife almost certainly would be exiled from Russia. Alexis's upbringing and care would be entrusted to other hands.

When the two Duma deputies arrived at nine that evening Nicholas had changed his mind. 'I have decided to renounce my throne. Until three o'clock today I thought I would abdicate in favour of my son Alexis, but now I have changed my decision in favour of my brother Michael. I trust you will understand the feelings of a father.' The Tsar then rose, took a new abdication document and left the room. Some time later he returned with the signed copy which he handed to the two emissaries. Shulgin was overcome with admiration and pity for this brave little man who was so amazingly controlled. 'Oh Your Majesty,' he blurted out, 'if you had done all this earlier, even as late as the summoning of the last Duma perhaps all that. . . . I could not finish,' wrote Shulgin. 'The Tsar looked at me in a curiously unaffected way. "Do you think it might have been avoided?"'[12]

Later, General Dubensky said that Nicholas 'abdicated from the throne of Russia as though he were handing over a squadron'. But the feelings were there, deep down. That night he wrote in his diary: 'For the sake of Russia and to keep the armies in the field, I decided to take this step. . . . Left Pskov at one in the morning. All around me I see treason, cowardice and deceit.'[12]

Might it have been avoided? Probably not. Despite the Emperor's ineffectualness, despite the Empress's tragic faith in Rasputin, despite their combined and medieval belief in saints and miracles and the divine right of kings, the revolution was not created by such relatively unimportant irritants. One thing stands out above all else. The revolution was precipitated by the mutiny of the army; and the army mutinied because it did not know what the war was about. 'The Russian peasant population is essentially pacific,' wrote General Knox, '. . . and never understood why it fought . . . a higher type of human animal was required to persevere to victory through the monotony of disaster. . . .' 'The soldiers did not want to fight any more,' wrote General Brusilov. 'The officer at once became an enemy in the soldiers' mind for he demanded continuance of the war; and in the soldiers' eyes represented the type of master in military uniform.' Even Kerensky, who did his best to continue the war, felt that Russia's participation had been a mistake. 'Russia had no really vital interests that made the war either inevitable or necessary. . . . Witte fully realized that Russia had everything to lose . . . with hardly anything to gain.'[13]

The Empress learned of her husband's abdication from two palace servants who returned from St Petersburg on foot on the afternoon of the sixteenth and said that leaflets were being distributed announcing the news. She flatly refused to believe it until the Grand Duke Paul arrived and confirmed the report. He added that the Grand Duke Michael had also abdicated, as there was so much hostility towards the Romanovs that the provisional government could not guarantee his life.

Lili Dehn heard agitated voices from the next room; then the Empress came in, 'her face distorted in agony, her eyes filled with tears'. 'She tottered rather than walked, and I rushed forward and supported her until she reached the writing table between the windows. She leaned heavily against it, and taking my hand in hers said brokenly: "*Abdiqué*". . . . I waited for her next words. They were hardly audible. "The poor dear . . . alone down there . . . what he must have suffered . . . and I was not there to console him."[14]

Five days later General Kornilov, the newly-appointed commander of the Petrograd garrison, arrived at the palace to tell the Empress that her husband would be returning from Mogilev next day. He introduced Captain Kotsebue, the new palace commander 'who must be obeyed', and informed her that all the palace entrances would be sealed except for the main doorway and the kitchen passage. As soon as Kornilov had left, the Empress sent for Gilliard and asked him if he would tell the Tsarevich about the Tsar's abdication – she would tell the girls herself. Alexis was in his room still recovering from measles, and Gilliard gently began by saying that the Tsar would not be returning to Mogilev since he was tired of being commander-in-chief. Alexis loved visiting headquarters, and was greatly moved.

'You know, your father does not want to be Tsar any more, Alexis Nikolaevich.'
'What! Why?'
'He is very tired and has had a lot of trouble lately.'
'Oh yes! Mother told me they had stopped his train when he wanted to come here. But won't Papa be Tsar again afterwards?'
'I then told him that the Tsar had abdicated in favour of the Grand Duke Michael who had also renounced the throne.'
'But who's going to be Tsar then?'
'I don't know. Perhaps nobody now.'
Not a word about himself. Not a single allusion to his rights as the heir. He was very red and agitated . . . then he said:
'But if there isn't a Tsar who's going to govern Russia?'
I explained that a Provisional Government had been formed. . . .[15]

Alexandra was with Alexis when she heard the Tsar's car on the drive. She ran downstairs and along the long corridors and threw herself into his arms. Nicholas was self-possessed and smiling. After his abdication he had gone to Army Headquarters to say goodbye to his men. The Dowager Empress, who was living in Kiev, had arrived by train and spent three days with him. Nicholas and Alexandra walked back to their private apartments with great composure. But when the door closed behind them the Tsar clasped his wife and wept like a child.

Now the imperial family were prisoners in their own palace. The new palace guard of rough young soldiers, controlled by three inept officers who were frightened of their men, were not in the palace grounds to guard the inhabitants but to restrict them. The period of transition with its inevitable humiliations was painful to everyone, but particularly to the small band of loyal courtiers who remained at their posts. A heartbreaking incident occurred the morning after the Tsar's arrival. The Empress went into Anna Vyrubova's room and told her that Nicholas had broken down for only a few minutes; now he was in complete control again. Since General Kornilov had given permission for the family to take exercise in the park, he had gone for a walk. 'Come to the window and see,' she said.

Never, [wrote Anna] while I live shall I forget what we saw – with him was his faithful friend Prince Dolgorouky, and surrounding them were six soldiers, say rather six hooligans, armed with rifles. With their fists and with the butts of their guns they pushed the Emperor this way and that as though he were some wretched vagrant they were baiting in a country road. 'You can't go there, *Gospodin Polkovnik* (Mr Colonel).' 'We don't permit you to walk in that direction, *Gospodin Polkovnik*' 'Stand back when you are commanded, *Gospodin Polkovnick*.'[16] With great dignity the Emperor merely looked at his tormentors and turned and walked back to the palace.

Nicholas and his guards at Tsarskoe Selo, March 1917.

There were many other unpleasant moments, carefully recorded by Anna. As she passed the Tsarevich's open door she saw his sailor–attendant – the man who had been his nurse and companion for ten years – sprawled in a chair shouting at the boy. 'Insolently he bawled at the boy whom he had formerly loved and cherished, to bring him this or that, to perform any menial services. Dazed and apparently only half conscious of what he was being forced to do the child moved about trying to obey.'[16] Derevenko left the palace, but Nagorny, the other sailor–attendant, remained.

Despite it all, the family managed to maintain a sense of humour. Nicholas began to joke about being addressed as an 'Ex-Emperor', and Alexandra copied him, saying: 'Don't call me an Empress any more, I'm only an Ex.' Once, Nicholas made everyone laugh when he tried to carve a ham that clearly had seen better days. 'This may have been a ham once,' he said, 'but now its only an ex.'

Nicholas found it more difficult to joke about the slovenly appearance of the palace guard. They walked about unshaven with their hair uncombed and their boots filthy. However they had to laugh when one of the guards on duty in front of the palace suddenly decided that standing at his post was too tiring and fetched a gilt chair from the drawing-room. 'I remarked', wrote Baroness Buxhoevden, 'that the man only wanted cushions to complete the picture. There was evidently telepathy ... for when we looked out again, he had actually got some sofa cushions ... and with a footstool under his feet was reading the papers, a discarded rifle at his feet.'[17]

It soon became apparent that the Palace Guard was more interested in young Alexis than anyone else. They tramped through the palace as they pleased, their heavy boots resounding through rooms and corridors. Somehow they found the nursery floor and Gilliard suddenly found himself facing ten of them.

'We want to see the Heir,' they said.

'He is in bed and can't be seen.'

'And the others?'

'They are also unwell.'

'And where is the Tsar?'

'I don't know; but don't hang around here. There must be no noise because of the invalids.'[18] Nodding, the men tiptoed away, murmuring to each other.

During the first week the fiery, deeply humane Alexander Kerensky came to see them. He drove up in one of the palace cars that he had commandeered and told Count Benckendorff that he had arrived 'to see how you live here, to inspect your palace and to talk to Nicholas Alexandrovich'. The real truth of the matter was that the Petrograd press had been inflaming the public with lurid tales of the Grand Duchesses' lovers, of gargantuan orgies at the palace of Alexandra's bloodthirsty treachery. As a result the Soviet had angrily demanded that Nicholas and Alexandra be thrown into the Fortress of St

Pierre Gilliard and one of the guards at Tsarskoe Selo.

Peter and St Paul, to await trial. 'I refuse to be the Murat of the Russian Revolution,' Kerensky had bravely replied; and now he found himself responsible for their safety. First it was essential to search the palace so that he could deny the current allegations of extravagance and espionage.

The family was lined up near a window in the drawing-room waiting to receive him. Everyone was nervous, including Kerensky.

A man of medium height in military kit, [wrote Kerensky] ... walked forward to meet me with a slight, peculiar smile. It was the Emperor ... he stopped in confusion. He did not know what to do, he did not know how I would act. ...

In a flash, instinctively, I knew the exact position; the family's ... fear at finding itself alone with a revolutionary whose objects in bursting in on it were unknown.

With an answering smile I hurriedly walked over to the Emperor, shook hands and sharply said 'Kerensky' as I always do by way of introduction. . . . Nicholas II gave my hand a firm grasp . . . and smiling once again, led me to his family.[19]

Kerensky's men searched all the rooms, and arrested Lili Dehn and Anna Vyrubova whom they took with them. Lili was released the next day but poor, crippled Anna, whose name had been so traduced that it had become a by-word for sexual depravity and treason, was thrown into the Fortress prison for five months. Luckily she was examined by an Investigating Committee which saw that the charges were unfounded and ordered her release. Kerensky appeared several times more to question both the Emperor and Empress on the parts they had played. Alexandra told him that her husband always discussed everything with her; of course they talked about the ministerial appointments, of course she expressed her views. Kerensky grew to respect both of them, the Empress for her honesty, the Emperor for his affability. Yet he was fascinated by the differences between them.

The Tsar and Tsarina, [he wrote] presented a complete contrast in every trifling detail; in smile, in bearing, in small mannerisms, in their attitude to people; in word, still more in thought. . . . The Tsar spoke; but it was the meaning of the Tsarina's silence that was more clearly apparent to me. By the side of a pleasant, somewhat awkward Colonel of the Guards, very ordinary except for a pair of wonderful blue eyes, stood a born Empress, proud, unbending, fully conscious of her right to rule.[20]

As the days passed the greatest strain for the family lay in wondering what would happen next. 'There was talk of our imminent transfer to England,' wrote Pierre Gilliard. 'Yet the days passed and our departure was always being postponed.' The Tsar suspected that the government was being thwarted by the Soviet. Yet the true story was much shabbier. The Provisional Government had requested asylum for the imperial family in early March. On the twenty-second of that month a Cabinet meeting was held in London at which it was agreed to make the offer. The invitation was extended not for humanitarian reasons but expediency. If the Tsar were safely in England, so the argument ran, Russian army leaders would not attempt a counter-revolution and thus preclude Russia's participation in the war.

No sooner had the invitation been sent to Petrograd than King George V began to regret it. On 6 April his secretary, Lord Stamfordham, wrote to the Foreign Secretary telling of the King's concern about the remarks Labour MPs were making in the House, not to mention the flood of critical letters he was receiving from Labour clubs. The King wondered if some other plan could not be made? By the afternoon of the same day, the King's alarm had increased still further and he instructed his secretary to dash off a second, even more vehement communication to the Foreign Minister.

The King wishes me to write again on the subject of my letter this morning. He begs you to represent to the PM that from all he hears and reads in the press, the residence in the country of an ex-emperor and empress would be strongly resented by the public and would undoubtedly compromise the position of the King and Queen.

Nicholas II with his cousin, King George V of England. In 1917 there were plans afoot in England to rescue the imperial family from Russia, but they were abandoned for political reasons.

Buchanan [the British Ambassador in Petrograd] ought to be instructed to tell Miliukov [the Russian Foreign Secretary] that the opposition to the Emperor and Empress coming here is so strong that one must be allowed to withdraw from the consent previously given to the Russian Government proposal.[21]

The refusal, of course, was the ultimate responsibility of the Prime Minister. But Lloyd George could scarcely override the King, when it not only concerned a brother monarch and his consort, but two close relations for whom he professed great fondness. Yet what makes George v's letter particularly shameful is the fact that through two and a half years of terrible fighting the Tsar had been Britain's faithful ally. Obviously George v's son, the Duke of Windsor, was not aware of the part his father played for he wrote that there was a very real bond between the two men. 'It hurt my father that Britain had not raised a finger to save his cousin Nicky. "Those politicians", he used to say. "If it had been one of their kind, they would have acted fast enough. But merely because the poor man was an emperor. . . ."'[22]

On 16 April 1917 – shortly after King George's protest – Lenin arrived back in Russia accompanied by his wife and nineteen fellow Bolsheviks. Berlin gave them permits to travel through Germany, as Winston Churchill put it, 'in a sealed train like a plague of bacillus'. The Petrograd Bolsheviks greeted their exiled leader, who had not set foot in Russia for ten years, with bands and banners. Among the welcoming committee on the platform were Molotov and two comrades just released from Siberian exile – Kamenev and Stalin. The Bolsheviks had ensconced themselves in the palace of Mathilde Kschessinska, the ballet dancer of Nicholas's bachelor days.

From the balcony Lenin made a number of impromptu speeches castigating the Provisional Government, urging the peasants to appropriate the land, the workers to take over the factories, the army to stop fighting and 'to fraternize with the enemy'. He repeated these extravagant commands the following night at the All Russian Conference of Soviets, dominated by Mensheviks and Social Revolutionaries. Many people in the audience, including Plekhanov who sat in his chair old and spent, had opposed Lenin bitterly in the past, and once again were amazed and indignant at what he was saying. Even Stalin and Kamenev were startled, since they were proceeding very cautiously, advocating support of the government in its determination to continue the war, and a merger between Bolsheviks and Mensheviks.

Some of the audience began to laugh at Lenin's harangue, and one man shouted: 'That is the raving of a lunatic.' Others were whistling and shouting so loudly that the speaker had to shout to be heard. 'Lenin was a hopeless failure with the Soviet yesterday,' wrote Miliukov, the Foreign Secretary, with relish. 'He was compelled to leave the room amidst a storm of booing. He will never survive it.' But in May a new and vibrant wind caught the sails of Lenin's ship. Leon Trotsky arrived from New York, where he had been living, severed his allegiance to former parties, and threw in his lot with the Bolsheviks.

Lenin and Trotsky worked hand in hand to achieve two immediate aims: control of the All Russian Soviet and overthrow of the Provisional Government. Since the Soviet was dominated by Mensheviks and Social Revolutionaries who outvoted the Bolsheviks by five to one, the two men decided to concentrate first on the government. They attacked the ministers as a bourgeois, liberal group of capitalist lackeys. Unfortunately the government not only had misread the causes of the revolution but was mistaken about the future. The ministers were under the impression that with the ineptitudes of the Tsarist rule eradicated, they would be able to win over the masses with a fairly simple, radical programme of reform. Nothing was further from the truth. Lenin knew the magic formula and continued his diatribe against the war. In May, when Miliukov blundered with a clumsy order to resume hostilities, he was howled out of office. Soon after, Guchkov and Prince Lvov were forced to resign.

Kerensky took over as Prime Minister and War Minister, and for a short time managed to handle the war question with more subtlety. Russia was desperately in need of credit and America said flatly: 'No war, no loans.' Largely on this argument, he persuaded the All Russian Soviet to pass a motion in favour of continuing hostilities. The army now had plenty of weapons and ammunition and opened up against the Austrians in Galicia at the end of June. The troops advanced for two weeks, then the Germans stepped in and brought the Russians to a halt. At this point the 'Soldiers' Committees' stepped in. These groups had been established by the Petrograd Soviet a few weeks after the Tsar's abdication in a famous military command known as 'Order No 1'. No decisions could be taken without committees which had the right to organize in every company in the army. The committees now came to the conclusion that in view of German intervention it was 'not wise' to proceed with their offensive. The enemy took advantage of the long pause, and attacked and routed the Russians along the entire front.

At this point the Petrograd Bolsheviks organized a massive parade through the streets of the capital. Half a million men carried banners shrieking: 'Down with the War.' Kerensky retaliated by circulating hundreds of leaflets among soldiers and workmen, declaring that Lenin was an enemy agent who had returned to Russia with German connivance in order to stir up trouble so that the German army could advance with the minimum resistance. The Russian masses were illiterate and unimaginative and believed whatever they were told – until they had time to consult their own self-interests. The idea that Lenin was making a fool of them infuriated them, and their loyalty swung away from the Bolsheviks and back to the Provisional Government, which at least had promised them a Constituent Assembly based on universal suffrage. Lenin fled to Finland on a locomotive, disguised as a fireman, and Trotsky and Kamenev gave themselves up and were sent to prison.

'The Bolsheviks are after me,' Kerensky announced cheerfully to Nicholas II, 'then they'll be after you.' He decided that the imperial family should leave Tsarskoe Selo for a place far removed from the capital without delay. The Tsar hoped for Livadia but the destination proved to be the little town of Tobolsk in Siberia. Apparently Kerensky secretly hoped that he eventually could move the family to Japan, from whence they could journey to the West.

On 13 August the Emperor and Empress, five children and two dogs, climbed aboard a comfortable train. They were accompanied by thirty servants including three cooks, four kitchenmaids, ten footmen, and six parlourmaids. Accompanying them was the kindly officer in charge of the guard, Colonel Kobylinsky, whose three hundred soldiers would be following in another train. Also with them were Prince Dolgorouky, Dr Botkin, Pierre Gilliard, General Tatishchev, and several other courtiers. The train was marked 'Japanese Red Cross' and flew Japanese flags; when it entered a station all the blinds were pulled down.

At the end of four days the party reached the town of Tiumen where Rasputin had been taken to hospital after his knife wound. Here the party was transferred to a steamer, the *Rus*, and for two days travelled up the Tura River. Curiously enough, they passed Rasputin's village, Pokrovskoe, and saw his two-storied house, built as a present from the Grand Duchess Militsa, dominating the hill.

At Tobolsk, the family was moved into a large white mansion which once had served as the governor's residence. The courtiers and servants were given accommodation across the street. Although a barricade was erected around the house to prevent passers-by from staring at the inmates, Colonel Kobylinsky did not insist on rigid discipline. He even allowed the prisoners to attend mass at the church next door. They always walked through two long lines of soldiers, behind which the townspeople gathered, many of them crossing themselves or falling on their knees. Soon the prisoners were receiving parcels of food and clothing smuggled in to them from the local inhabitants; before long they were managing to pass letters surreptitiously to members of the staff, which were secretly taken to the capital.

At first life was monotonous, but not unhappy. The girls occupied themselves in acting French plays; in reading, sewing and studying; and the Empress even took German lessons since she was beginning to forget her native tongue. What pleased the family most, however, was the fact that little Alexis was remarkably well.

The anger against Lenin was nothing more than a flash in the pan. Despite his attitude to the Germans he had what the people wanted. Lenin's slogan 'Peace, Bread and Land' promised to satisfy the most crying wants of the vast peasant population. The Government's appeal – and even the exhortations of Mensheviks and Social Revolutionaries – to fight for 'freedom and revolution' meant nothing to them. Lenin's genius lay in his ability to

Alexis with his spaniel, Joy.

A revolutionary procession passing the Kornilov house in Tobolsk,
where the imperial family were imprisoned.

harness the class war and the rule of the proletariat with the country's
immediate needs and desires, and to focus and canalize the support of the
most illiterate and ignorant with his simple banner: 'All Power to the
Soviets'.

Lenin's comeback was aided by General Kornilov, the newly appointed
commander-in-chief. The General sensed that the Provincial Government

was losing ground to the Soviet and decided to march on Petrograd with a cavalry corps and set up a dictatorship. Kerensky was to be given a place in the new Government but Kornilov would assume the leading role. Unfortunately Kornilov did not plan his *coup d'état* with any finesse. Later someone remarked that he had 'the heart of a lion and the brain of a sheep'. His mistake was to tell his plans to Kerensky, for Kerensky still regarded himself as a socialist.

Surprisingly, Kerensky turned for help to the Bolsheviks, who had been reviling him for weeks. They eagerly accepted, called out the Red Guards, and when the government depots distributed arms, the Bolsheviks grabbed most of them. However, the weapons were not needed for the Kornilov *coup d'état* disintegrated almost as soon as it started. When the General's troops reached the capital they began to fraternize with the Soviet mutineers, which brought the whole affair to an abrupt close.

Kerensky had made a fatal blunder for which there was no reprieve. The truth was that he was no match for Lenin. The latter was a professional revolutionary who had spent a lifetime thinking out how to implement his Marxist theories. Kerensky, on the other hand, was an emotional demagogue who claimed to be a 'labour man' but once the autocracy was smashed did not know what direction to take. 'A *petit braggart*', Lenin said: 'A noisy lawyer', pronounced Sukhanov. 'Kerensky was not a revolutionary,' wrote Trotsky, 'He merely hung around the revolution.' '... He had no theoretical preparation, no political schooling, no ability to think, no political will. The place of these qualities was occupied by a nimble susceptibility; an inflammable temperament, and that kind of eloquence which operates neither upon mind nor will but upon the nerves.'[23]

A few weeks later Lenin gained a majority within the Petrograd Soviet. Now he was ready to make an immediate lunge for the final power. 'History will not forgive us if we do not take power now ... to delay is a crime.' On 23 October he slipped back into Russia and the Bolshevik Central Committee voted overwhelmingly that 'the time was ripe ... for insurrection.'

On 6 November the Bolsheviks struck. The first day they occupied railway stations, bridges, the telephone exchange, the post office, banks and other government buildings. There was no fighting, no resistance. On the morning of the seventh, Kerensky left for the front in an open touring car to try to rustle up some military support. He never returned, and after several months in hiding escaped from Russia with the help of the British agent, Bruce Lockhart. The Ministers of the Provincial Government were meeting in the Winter Palace and remained in session for nearly thirty-six hours. Thirty or forty shells whistled over the building but only two of them found a mark, doing little damage except to bring down some plaster. Since it was becoming obvious that no aid would be forthcoming they finally dissolved the meeting and slipped away. The Bolsheviks had control of Russia.

At first the change of government did not affect the prisoners in Tobolsk.

209

The Tsar at Tobolsk, sawing wood with Pierre Gilliard.

The Empress wrote regularly to Anna Vyrubova, who had been released from prison, telling her the small events of the day; how she sewed, read the Bible, gave the children lessons in theology, and, above all, how marvellous was the behaviour of the Tsar. Nicholas's tendency to fatalism served him well for he suffered his fall from power with astonishing composure. His conscience was clear. He did not hold himself to blame in any way for losing his throne or for what had happened since. His tribulations were God's will and therefore must be endured without complaint. Alexandra wrote on 10 December 1917:

I am so sad because they [Nicholas and the children] are allowed no walks except before the house and behind a high fence. But at least they have fresh air, and we are grateful for everything. He is simply marvellous. Such meekness while all the time suffering for his country. A real marvel. The others are all good and brave and uncomplaining, and Alexis is an angel. He and I dine *à deux* and generally lunch so, but sometimes down with the others.'[24]

Alexandra had not been able to adjust herself to her new position with the same ease as Nicholas. She still refused to believe that the peasants – 'the real people' as she called them – had turned against the Tsar, and regarded both the Duma and the Bolshevik *coups d'états* as engineered by ambitious traitors. For months she dreamed of a popular uprising that would put them back on the throne – or at the very least, of a spirited rescue that would free them from their gaolers. Only gradually did she come to accept the new circumstances as the fate to which her family must bow. In order to fortify herself she turned increasingly to religion, until at times she seemed to be living in a world of inner thought, totally divorced from material surroundings.

Even the worsened conditions inflicted by the Bolsheviks did not disturb her. As soon as Prime Minister Kerensky departed the money stopped coming from Petrograd to pay the soldiers of the guard, and the Tsar's household expenses. Count Benckendorff assailed the various ministries in the capital to no avail; finally he rustled up 200,000 roubles from friends, but the money disappeared on the way to Siberia.

I am knitting stockings for the small one [Alexandra wrote in December]. He [Alexis] asked for a pair as all his are in holes. Mine are warm and thick like the ones I gave the wounded, do you remember? I make everything now. Father's trousers are torn and darned, the girls' underlinen in rags. Dreadful, is it not? I have grown quite grey. Anastasia, to her despair, is now very fat, as Marie was, round and fat to the waist, with short legs. I do hope she will grow. Olga and Tatiana are both thin, but their hairs grows beautifully so that they can go without scarves [the girls' hair was cut short when they had measles]. . . . I find myself writing in English, I don't know why. Be sure and burn all these letters as at any time your house may be searched again.[24]

In January the family was put on soldiers' rations which meant the end of all luxuries such as coffee, butter and sugar. To the prisoners this was a small sacrifice in view of the horrors that were taking place in Russia. Alexandra's religious fervour enabled her to preserve a deep faith in the Russian people. Whatever reservations one may have of Nicholas and Alexandra as autocratic rulers, the coldest heart cannot fail to admire their spiritual splendour in adversity. Everything was there: courage, magnanimity, faith. Indeed, some of the qualities that destroyed them in power sustained them in defeat. This new-found serenity shines from Alexandra's letters with flashes of deep understanding and beauty.

9 January 1918
. . . Believe dear, that God will yet save our beloved country. . . . The reign of terror is not yet over, and it is the suffering of the innocent which nearly kills us. What do people live on now that everything is taken from them, their homes, their incomes, their money? We must have sinned terribly for our Father in Heaven to punish us so frightfully. But firmly and unfalteringly believe that in the end He will save us. The strange thing about the Russian character is that it can so suddenly change to evil, cruelty, and unreason, and can as suddenly change back again. . . . Russians are in reality big ignorant children. . . .

Grand Duchess Tatiana at Tobolsk, working in the garden.

2 March 1918.

... Life here is nothing – eternity is everything, and what we are doing is preparing our souls for the Kingdom of Heaven. Thus nothing, after all, is terrible, and if they do take everything from us they cannot take our souls. . . .[24]

On 3 March the Russians signed the Treaty of Brest-Litovsk which brought peace with Germany – but at a stiff price. Nicholas was very depressed. 'It is such a disgrace for Russia,' he told Gilliard, 'and amounts to suicide. I should never have thought the Emperor Wilhelm and the German Government could stoop to shake hands with those miserable traitors. But I'm sure they will get no good from it; it won't save them from ruin!'[25]

Alexandra very often was in a state bordering on religious exaltation and the news of the peace treaty did not upset her as much as it did her husband. '... How I love my country, with all its faults,' she wrote to Anna. 'It grows dearer and dearer to me and I thank God daily that He allowed us to remain here and did not send us further away. Believe in the people, darling. The nation is strong, and young, and as soft as wax. Just now it is in bad hands, and darkness and anarchy reigns. But the King of Glory will come and will save, strengthen, and give wisdom to the people, who are now deceived.'[26]

In April Alexis, who had been well all winter, fell and hurt himself and had his worst haemorrhage since Spala. Alexandra sat with him day and night while the child screamed with pain and often implored God to let him die. He became so wasted and yellow it seemed impossible that he could live, but finally the bleeding stopped. His leg was so contracted that it would be months before he could walk again.

In the middle of the attack, on 22 April, a new commissar arrived. Yakovlev was in his thirties, very polite. He told the family that they would have to go on a long trip – destination secret. Alexis was too ill to move, so it was finally agreed that Nicholas would depart alone. Alexandra still laboured under the impression that Nicholas's Divine Right gave him great authority and she became distraught. 'They're going to try to force his hand by making him anxious about his family,' she told Gilliard. 'The Tsar is necessary to them; they feel that he alone represents Russia – I ought to be at his side at the time of trial ... but the boy is still so ill. ...'[27] In the end the Grand Duchesses persuaded her to go with Nicholas, assuring her that they would give Alexis every care. Grand Duchess Marie accompanied her mother as a companion; Prince Dolgorouky and Dr Botkin were allowed to go, also a valet, a footman and a maid, and eight soldiers of the guard.

The trip was a nightmare of discomfort. The prisoners had to travel 200 miles in the bitter cold in peasant carts known as *tarantasses*. These vehicles consisted of a large wicker basket hung with two long poles which took the place of springs. There were no seats and the passengers had to sit or lie on the floor. The journey took forty hours. The roads were treacherous, wheels broke and several times the horses were up to their chests in water crossing the rivers.

The horrific journey ended at Tiumen. Here the imperial prisoners were transferred to a first-class carriage on a train. They could not know, of course, that their fate was being directed by Sverdlov, a member of Lenin's inner cabinet; and that Sverdlov was playing the game of duplicity so dear to the Russian heart – a game of which even Yakovlev had no knowledge. The Treaty of Brest-Litovsk had made the Germans, very fleetingly, the masters of Russia, and the new ambassador, Count Mirbach, had assured the loyal courtier, Count Benckendorff, that he would do his best to protect the Emperor's person – hence Yakovlev's instructions to bring the imperial family to Moscow.

But secretly the Bolsheviks, led by Lenin and Sverdlov, had no intention of allowing the Romanovs to escape. By an 'inspired leak' the Ural Soviet, a

The Empress's drawing-room at Tobolsk.

violently extreme group, learned what was happening, and when Yakovlev tried to circumvent their headquarters at Ekaterinburg by ordering the train tp proceed to Omsk they sent frantic telegrams to their comrades to block its progress. As a result, the train was surrounded by troops sixty miles from Omsk. When Yakovlev finally got in touch with Sverdlov in Moscow the latter feigned chagrin, adding that now there was no alternative but to take the prisoners to Ekaterinburg and hand them over to the Ural praesidium.

The local soviet seemed to know in advance how the story would end, for several days earlier they had ordered the town's most prosperous merchant, M.M.Ipatiev, to vacate his spacious, two-storey residence within twenty-four hours. They then summoned a group of workmen to block out the windows with white paint and to build a high wooden fence around the edifice, which was aptly named 'The House of Special Purpose'. This was the dwelling into which the Emperor and Empress and the Grand Duchess Marie were relegated on 30 April. In the second half of May, to their great joy, they were joined by the three other Grand Duchesses and Alexis, who, although he was pronounced well enough to travel, still could not walk. Accompanying him was his sailor-nurse, Nagorny, and Dr Botkin. Other

*At Ekaterinburg conditions were far worse. The Grand Duchesses'
bedroom in the House of Special Purpose.*

members of the imperial retinue – Baroness Buxhoevden, Dr Derevenko,
Sydney Gibbes, an English tutor, and Pierre Gilliard – were not permitted to
take up residence in the Ipatiev house, but lived forlornly in a railway
carriage at the station. However a cook, a footman and a fourteen-year-old
kitchen boy were allowed to attend the prisoners, as well as Demidova, the
Empress's maid. Dr Botkin was also given permission to live with the family.

The new guards were hard-line Communists – rough factory workers who
aped the behaviour of their drunken, foul-mouthed leader. They refused to
allow the Grand Duchesses to shut their doors, and insisted on accompanying them to the lavatory on the playful pretext of keeping them under strict
guard. They pilfered the girls' suitcases, drew obscene pictures on the walls,
and made a point of taking their meals with the family in order to shock them
by plunging their dirty hands into the communal dishes. When the sailor
Nagorny objected to their stealing Alexis's ikons he was sent to prison and
speedily shot as a counter-revolutionary.

On 4 July these guards were dismissed and their places taken by a squad of
ten polite and detached men referred to as 'the Letts'. All of them were
members of the secret police, the Bolshevik Cheka. Five were Magyar

prisoners-of-war, the other five Russians. They were headed by Jacob Yurovsky, a former watchmaker in Tomsk. Twelve days after their arrival, they ordered the fourteen-year-old kitchen boy out of the house for no apparent reason. That night Yurovsky awakened the family at midnight, telling them that the White Army was approaching Ekaterinburg. They were to dress quickly and to come downstairs, because a fleet of cars would soon be arriving to take them away. Nicholas appeared first, carrying Alexis, and soon the whole family was assembled in the small basement room. The Emperor and Empress were given chairs. Behind Alexandra stood the four girls, and next to them the cook, the valet, Dr Botkin and the ladies' maid, Demidova, who carried a cushion concealing a collection of imperial jewels sewn into the feathers. Yurovsky re-entered the room, followed by his men, all heavily armed. 'Your relatives have tried to save you,' he said. 'They have failed and we must now shoot you.'

Nicholas was killed by the first bullet from Yurovsky's revolver and Alexandra a second later, before she could even make the sign of the cross. In the hail of lead that followed three of the Grand Duchesses died quickly, and so did Dr Botkin and two of the servants. Poor Demidova survived the first round and the men fell on her with bayonets. Then Alexis groaned and opened his eyes. Yurovsky stepped forwards and fired into his ear. Anastasia was only stunned and sat up screaming. Like Demidova, she met her death as half a dozen bayonets were driven into her body.

Before leaving Tobolsk, eleven weeks earlier, the Empress had written prophetically to Anna Vyrubova: 'The atmosphere around us is electrified. We fear that a storm is approaching but we know that God is merciful. . . . Our souls are at peace. Whatever happens will be through God's Will.'

Epilogue

Although the execution of the Emperor was easy to defend, Lenin was not prepared to admit to the massacre of the family, which he felt might shock people and turn them against the Bolshevik regime. Consequently, on 20 July 1918, the Tsar's death was announced in Moscow by Sverdlov, followed by a statement that the rest of the imperial family had been removed from Ekaterinburg to a place of safety. The Ural soviet had instructions to conceal all traces of the massacre, and Voikov, a member of the local praesidium who later became ambassador to Poland, was so pleased with his handiwork that he boasted: 'The world will never know what we did with them.'

At first it seemed as though he had prophesied correctly, for although the White armies over-ran Ekaterinburg eight days after the killing, no one could discover what had happened to the family. Although the basement room in Ipatiev's house had been scrubbed clean there was no way to disguise the bullet holes and bayonet thrusts. People had died there, but who and how many? In January 1919 Admiral Kolchak, head of the White government in Siberia, appointed a trained jurist, Nicholas Sokolov, to carry out an investigation, and the Tsarevich's tutors, Sydney Gibbes and Pierre Gilliard, remained in Ekaterinburg to assist him.

Gradually the mystery was solved. After the murder the bodies had been placed on a truck and driven to a clearing in the forest, fourteen miles away, near a mineshaft guarded by four pine trees known as 'The Four Brothers'. The corpses were stripped and hacked to pieces, the severed segments being thrown on to a bonfire which was continuously soaked in petrol and kept burning for three days. The bones that remained were dissolved in 400-lb drums of sulphuric acid that had been procured by Voikov. Because human skulls are difficult to destroy, it is generally believed that the heads were put in a sack and dumped into a swamp or river. The ashes and small remains were thrown into the pool at the bottom of the mineshaft where they were thought to be permanently hidden. Nevertheless from this pool evidence was collected that left the three men in no doubt as to what had happened. Among the many objects which they recovered were the belt buckles of both Tsar and Tsarevich; an emerald cross worn by the Empress, and a well manicured finger that probably belonged to the same owner; shoe buckles worn by the Grand Duchesses; the Empress's spectacle case; six sets of women's corsets; Dr Botkin's false teeth; small ikons worn by the girls; and the body of Jimmy, Anastasia's spaniel.

Human beings love mystery, and often only an irrefutable corpse can put an end to speculation. In this case the fact that the bodies of the imperial family were never found has resulted in a spate of allegations and conjectures that has persisted for over sixty years. Shortly after the murder a boy claiming to be the Tsarevich was interviewed by Gilliard; he finally broke down and admitted that he was an imposter. Dozens of Anastasias have appeared, the most controversial being the lady known as Anna Anderson. However, despite a mountain of affidavits both for and against her claim, it is significant that not one of the three women most closely related to the real Anastasia – her grandmother and two aunts (the Dowager Empress and the Grand Duchesses Xenia and Olga) – was convinced of Anna's authenticity. As members of the Romanov family have told the author: 'Imagine our joy if the real Anastasia had appeared. How could anyone imagine we would refuse to accept her if we believed in her identity.'

Recently a book has been published claiming that only Nicholas II – and possibly his heir, Alexis – were shot; and that the Empress and her daughters were removed to another part of Russia. The story originated in December 1918 when a *New York Times* reporter, Ackerman, quoted as his source Parfin Domnin, who claimed to have served the Tsar for twenty-two years and to have accompanied him into exile. The report did not create the stir that Ackerman expected, as no one by the name of Domnin had ever been on the Emperor's staff.

In *The File on the Tsar* the authors argue that pressure from Germany in the summer of 1918 influenced Lenin to order the removal from Ekaterinburg of the Empress and her daughters – no one is sure what became of Alexis. However, it must be pointed out that the Kaiser, nearing the collapse of his own dynasty, had not been in charge of Germany's destinies for many months. Hindenburg and Ludendorff were the supreme warlords who had dictated the peace treaty with Russia that March. It seems very unlikely that these two famous soldiers, fighting for the very life of their country, should have found the time to occupy themselves with the fate of the hostile Empress Alexandra because she happened to have been born a German. The authors end their conjectures with the words: 'Access to the Kremlin archives remains a researcher's dream. The answers must be in there somewhere ... until then the truth about the Romanovs remains a casualty of history.'[1]

However, many people believe that the truth was told by two members of the Bolshevik Cheka squad who described the massacre; by the peasants who saw the fires burning near the mineshaft; and by Trotsky, who in his memoirs congratulated Lenin on the ruthless course he had followed. When Ekaterinburg fell to the Whites Trotsky asked Sverdlov:

'Oh yes, and where is the Tsar?'
'It's all over,' he answered. 'He has been shot.'
'And where is the family?'
'And the family along with him.'
'All of them?' I asked, apparently with a touch of surprise.
'All of them,' replied Sverdlov. . . .
'And who made the decision?' I asked.
'We decided in here. Ilyich [Lenin] believed that we shouldn't leave the Whites a

live banner to rally around, especially under the present difficult circumstances. . . .'

Actually the decision was not only expedient but necessary . . . to show that there was no turing back.[2]

The Dowager Empress and her daughters were luckier than Nicholas and his family. Accompanied by her elder daughter Xenia, and the Grand Duke Nicholas Nicolaevich, former Commander-in-Chief of the Russian Army, the seventy-two-year-old Empress Marie left Russian soil by way of Odessa on the British battleship *Marlborough* in April 1919. The Tsar's younger sister, the Grand Duchess Olga, and her second husband left that same spring from Novorossiysk in a British merchant ship for Turkey. The Grand Duchess Vladimir, widow of the Tsar's uncle, escaped from the Caucasus and arrived in Novorossiysk before Olga departed.

There had never been much love between Aunt Michen and my own family, [wrote Olga] but I felt proud of her. Disregarding peril and hardship, she stubbornly kept to all the trimmings of a bygone splendour and glory. And somehow she carried it off. When even generals found themselves lucky to find a horse-cart and an old nag to bring them to safety, Aunt Michen made a long journey in her own train. It was battered all right – but it was hers.'[1]

The Romanovs who did not survive included the Tsar's younger brother, the Grand Duke Michael, who was shot in Perm six days before the Ekaterinburg murder, and the Tsar's uncle, the Grand Duke Paul, who was shot in the fortress of St Peter and St Paul in January 1919. On 17 July, the day after the imperial massacre, the Tsarina's sister, the Grand Duchess Elizabeth, and the Grand Duke Sandro's brother, the Grand Duke Serge Mikhailovich, were brutally murdered along with a son of the Grand Duke Paul and the three sons of the Grand Duke Constantine.

The assassins of Rasputin – the Grand Duke Dimitri and Prince Youssoupov – escaped from Persia and Central Russia, and spent their lives in America and France. Among the politicians who managed to survive were Rodzianko, the last president of the Tsar's Duma, who made his way to Belgrade where he died in 1924, and Count Kokovtsov, Prince Lvov, Miliukov and Guchkov who all spent their lives in France. The Baroness Buxhoevden crossed Siberia and got to England; Anna Vyrubova made her way to Finland and lived to the age of eighty; Pierre Gilliard became a professor of French at Lausanne University in Switzerland. Generals Alexeiev and Kornilov died leading White Armies against the Reds; Generals Brusilov and Polivanov threw in their lot with the Bolsheviks. The ballet dancer Mathilde Kschessinska married one of the Grand Duchess Vladimir's sons, Prince Andrei, at Cannes in 1921.

Bibliographical Notes

Title, author, publisher, and place and date of publication are given in the first reference to each work. Subsequent references give full title only.

CHAPTER I

1. *The Vanished Pomps of Yesterday, Reminiscences of a British Diplomat,* Lord Frederick Hamilton (p. 120). Hodder and Stoughton, London, 1920.
2. *The Life of Benjamin Disraeli,* Vol. VI, W.F.Monypenny and G.E.Buckle (pp. 132–3). John Murray, London, 1920.
3. *Tolstoy,* Henri Troyat (p. 385). W.H.Allen, London, 1968.
4. *Once a Grand Duke,* Grand Duke Alexander Mikhailovich (p. 70). Cassell, London, 1932.
5. *Once a Grand Duke* (pp. 71–2).
6. *The Memoirs of Count Witte* (p. 39). Heinemann, London, 1921.
7. *The Letters of Tsar Nicholas and Empress Marie,* ed. Edward Bing (pp. 33–4). Ivor Nicholson and Watson, London, 1937.
8. *Once a Grand Duke* (pp. 188–9).
9. *Alexander III of Russia,* Charles Lowe (p. 348). Heinemann, London, 1895.
10. *Nicholas II : The Last of the Tsars,* Princess Catherine Radziwill (p. 47). Cassell, London, 1931.
11. *Alexander III of Russia* (p. 355).
12. *The Letters of Tsar Nicholas and Empress Marie* (p. 75).
13. *The Letters of Tsar Nicholas and Empress Marie* (p. 76).
14. *Once a Grand Duke* (p. 189).

CHAPTER 2

1. *The Last Grand Duchess,* Ian Vorres (pp. 67–8). Hutchinson, London, 1964.

2. *Three Who Made a Revolution,* Bertram D. Wolfe (p. 21). Thames and Hudson, London, 1956.
3. *The Intimate Life of the Last Tsarina,* Princess Catherine Radziwell. Cassell, London, 1929.
4. *Memories of the Russian Court,* Anna Vyrubova (pp. 21–2). Macmillan, New York, 1923.
5. *The Letters of Tsar Nicholas and Empress Marie* (p. 103).
6. *Nicholas II : The Last of the Tsars* (p. 98).
7. *Nicholas II : The Last of the Tsars* (pp. 105–7).
8. *Nicholas II : The Last of the Tsars* (pp. 102–3).
9. *Nicholas II : The Last of the Tsars* (p. 117).
10. *Once a Grand Duke* (p. 193).
11. *The Memoirs of Count Witte* (p. 182).
12. *The Intimate Life of the Last Tsarina* (pp. 75–6).
13. *Memories of the Russian Court* (pp. 4–5).
14. *At the Court of the Last Tsar,* A.A.Mossolov (p. 239). Methuen, London, 1935.
15. *Grosse Politik,* 23A, No. 7877 (p. 161).
16. *The Origins of the World War,* Sidney Fay (pp. 366–7). Macmillan, New York, 1929 and 1959.
17. *The Memoirs of Count Witte* (p. 117).
18. *The Letters and Friendships of Sir Cecil Spring Rice,* Vol. 1 (p. 425). Constable, London, 1929.
19. *The Crucifixion of Liberty,* Alexander Kerensky (p. 13). Arthur Barker, London, 1934.
20. *The Eclipse of Russia,* Dr E.J.Dillon (p. 133). Dent, London, 1918.
21. *Nicholas II : The Last of the Tsars* (p. 154).
22. *Nicholas II : The Last of the Tsars* (pp. 157–8).
23. *The Letters of Tsar Nicholas and Empress Marie* (pp. 187–8).
24. *The Russian Revolution,* Alan Moorehead (p. 72). Collins with Hamish Hamilton, London, 1958.
25. *The Letters of Tsar Nicholas and Empress Marie* (p. 179).
26. *The Letters of Tsar Nicholas and Empress Marie* (p. 188).
27. *At the Court of the Last Tsar* (p. 90).
28. *The Letters of Tsar Nicholas and Empress Marie* (pp. 91, 194 and 212).
29. *Out of My Past : The Memoirs of Count Kokovtsvov* (pp. 129–30). Stanford University Press, Stanford, California, 1935.
30. *At the Court of the Last Tsar* (p. 139).

CHAPTER 3
1. *The Real Tsaritsa,* Lili Dehn (pp. 39–40). Thornton Butterworth, London, 1922.
2. *At the Court of the Last Tsar,* A.A.Mossolov (p. 32).
3. *At the Court of the Last Tsar* (p. 36).
4. *Memories of the Russian Court,* Anna Vyrubova (p. 16).

5. *Nicholas and Alexandra,* Robert Massie (pp. 168–9). Gollancz, London, 1968.
6. *Thirteen Years at the Russian Court,* Pierre Gilliard (p. 26). Hutchinson, London, 1921.
7. *The Last Grand Duchess* (p. 138).
8. *The Last Grand Duchess* (pp. 142–3).
9. *At the Court of the Last Tsar* (p. 150).
10. *The Origins of the World War* (pp. 371–2).
11. *Grosse Politik,* 22 (p. 83f).
12. Report of Vesnitch, Serbian Minister in Paris.
13. *King Edward VII,* Sir Philip Magnus (p. 417). John Murray, London, 1964.
14. *The Letters of Tsar Nicholas and Empress Marie* (p. 236).
15. *King Edward VII* (p. 420).
16. *The Letters of Tsar Nicholas and Empress Marie* (p. 236).
17. *Lord Carnock,* Sir Harold Nicolson (p. 312). Constable, London, 1930.
18. *Once a Grand Duke* (p. 201).
19. *Out of My Past* (p. 167).
20. *Once a Grand Duke* (pp. 209–10).
21. *Thirteen Years at the Russian Court* (p. 52).
22. *The Russian Revolution* (p. 88).
23. *The Fall of the Russian Monarchy,* Sir Bernard Pares (p. 143). Jonathan Cape, London, 1939.
24. *The Letters of Tsar Nicholas and Empress Marie* (pp. 265–6).
25. *Out of My Past* (p. 283).
26. *The Fall of the Russian Monarchy* (pp. 146–7).
27. *The Russian Revolution* (pp. 87–8).
28. *Out of My Past* (p. 300).
29. *At the Court of the Last Tsar* (pp. 166–7).

CHAPTER 4
1. *Out of My Past* (p. 296).
2. *Memories of the Russian Court* (p. 35).
3. *Memories of the Russian Court* (p. 79).
4. *Memories of the Russian Court* (p. 8).
5. *Thirteen Years at the Russian Court* (pp. 42–3).
6. *The Letters of Tsar Nicholas and Empress Marie* (pp. 248 and 254).
7. *Nicholas II : The Last of the Tsars* (pp. 194–5).
8. *The Letters of Tsar Nicholas and Empress Marie* (p. 277).
9. *Memories of the Russian Court* (pp. 92–3).
10. *Fateful Years, 1904–1916,* Serge Sazonov (pp. 285–6). Jonathan Cape, London, 1928.
11. *Out of My Past* (pp. 345 and 348).
12. *The Crucifixion of Liberty* (p. 162).
13. *The Russian Revolution* (p. 106).

14. *Lenin,* Ralph Fox (p. 189). Gollancz, London, 1933.
15. *Memories of the Russian Court* (pp. 99–100 and 80).
16. *At the Court of the Last Tsar* (p. 247).
17. *Thirteen Years at the Russian Court* (p. 94).
18. *An Ambassador's Memoirs,* Vol. 1, Maurice Paleologue (pp. 22–3). Hutchinson, London, 1923–5.
19. *Recent Revelations of European Diplomacy,* G.P.Gooch (p. 207). Longmans, London, 1927.
20. *The Diary of Lord Bertie of Thame,* Vol. 1 (p. 1). Hodder and Stoughton, London, 1924.
21. *Thirteen Years at the Russian Court* (p. 100).
22. *The Fall of the Russian Monarchy* (p. 188).
23. *Memories of the Russian Court* (p. 106).
24. *Outbreak of the World War: German Documents collected by Karl Kautsky,* Nos 335 and 332. Carnegie Endowment, Oxford University Press, New York, 1924.
25. *Schilling's Diary,* trans. Major W.E.Bridge (p. 65). London, 1925.
26. *Memories of the Russian Court* (pp. 105–6).
27. *Forty Years of Diplomacy,* Baron Rosen (p. 172). George Allen and Unwin, London, 1922.
28. *The Memoirs of Count Witte.*

CHAPTER 5
1. *The Crucifixion of Liberty* (p. 175).
2. *An Ambassador's Memoirs,* Vol. 1 (pp. 62–3).
3. *With the Russian Army 1914–1917,* Vol 1, Sir Alfred Knox (p. 86). Hutchinson, London, 1921.
4. *With the Russian Army 1914–1917,* Vol. 1 (p. 92).
5. *Memories of the Russian Court* (pp. 109–10).
6. *Thirteen Years at the Russian Court* (p. 137).
7. *The End of the Russian Empire,* Michael Florinsky (p. 225). Carnegie Endowment, Yale University Press, New York, 1931.
8. *Memories of the Russian Court* (p. 121).
9. *The Fall of the Russian Monarchy* (p. 230).
10. *The Fall of the Russian Monarchy* (pp. 231–2).
11. *The End of the Russian Empire* (p. 76).
12. *The End of the Russian Empire* (p. 213).
13. *Letters of the Tsaritsa to the Tsar,* ed. Sir Bernard Pares (pp. 62–100). Duckworth, London, 1923.
14. *Letters of the Tsaritsa to the Tsar* (pp. 89, 97–8, 100 and 110).
15. *Letters of the Tsaritsa to the Tsar* (pp. 113–15).
16. *Letters of the Tsar to the Tsaritsa,* ed. Sir Bernard Pares (p. 104). Duckworth, London, 1923.
17. *Thirteen Years at the Russian Court* (pp. 155–6).
18. *Memories of the Russian Court* (pp. 169–70).

19. *An Ambassador's Memoirs*, Vol II (p. 166).
20. *Letters of the Tsaritsa to the Tsar* (pp. 439–40).
21. *Letters of the Tsaritsa to the Tsar.*
22. *Memories of the Russian Court* (p. 179).
23. *The Fall of the Russian Monarchy* (p. 399).
24. *The Reign of Rasputin,* M.V.Rodzianko (pp. 252–4). A.M.Philpot, London, 1927.
25. *With the Russian Army 1914–1917,* Vol. I (p. 34).
26. *My Mission to Russia,* Sir George Buchanan (pp. 42–5). Cassell, London, 1923.
27. *Once a Grand Duke* (pp. 314–15).
28. *The Reign of Rasputin* (p. 263).

CHAPTER 6
1. *The Fall of the Russian Monarchy* (p. 443).
2. *An Ambassador's Memoirs,* Vol. III (pp. 221–2).
3. *With the Russian Army 1914–1917,* Vol. II (pp. 554–5).
4. *The Fall of the Russian Monarchy* (p. 446).
5. *The Fall of the Russian Monarchy* (p. 451).
6. *The Fall of the Russian Monarchy* (p. 450).
7. *The Crucifixion of Liberty* (p. 244).
8. *The Real Tsaritsa* (p. 149).
9. *The Life and Tragedy of Alexandra Feodorovna, Empress of Russia,* Baroness Sophie Buxhoevden (p. 255). Longmans, London, 1928.
10. *The Murder of the Romanovs,* Paul Bulygin and Alexander Kerensky (pp. 90–2). Hutchinson, London, 1935.
11. *Thirteen Years at the Russian Court* (p. 195).
12. *The Fall of the Russian Monarchy* (pp. 468–9).
13. *The Crucifixion of Liberty* (pp. 167–8).
14. *The Real Tsaritsa* (p. 165).
15. *Thirteen Years at the Russian Court* (pp. 214–15).
16. *Memories of the Russian Court* (p. 213).
17. *The Life and Tragedy of Alexandra Feodorovna, Empress of Russia* (p. 284).
18. *Thirteen Years at the Russian Court* (p. 222).
19. *The Murder of the Romanovs* (p. 122).
20. *The Crucifixion of Liberty* (pp. 147–8).
21. PRO/Foreign Office 800/250.
22. *A King's Story,* HRH The Duke of Windsor (p. 129). Cassell, London, 1951.
23. *History of the Russian Revolution,* Leon Trotsky (p. 201). Gollancz, London, 1933–4.
24. *Memories of the Russian Court* (pp. 311–12, 316, 318 and 333).
25. *Thirteen Years at the Russian Court* (p. 257).
26. *Memories of the Russian Court* (p. 336).

27. *Thirteen Years at the Russian Court* (pp. 260–1).
28. *Memories of the Russian Court* (pp. 341–2).

EPILOGUE
1. *The File on the Tsar*, Anthony Summers and Tom Mangold, Gollancz, London, 1976.
2. *History of the Russian Revolution*.
3. *The Last Grand Duchess* (p. 167).

Acknowledgements

The following individuals, museums and agencies have provided illustrations and given their permission to reproduce them. Numbers in *italics* refer to colour illustrations.

103, 107 below Bildarchiv; 20, 65 Mary Evans Picture Library; *41, 42 above, middle and below*, 49, 86, 106 below, 127, 141, 142 below, *144*, 171, 177, 201, 208, 210, 214, 215 George Gibbes; 22–3, 81, *117, 118, 143*, Victor Kennett; frontispiece, 10, 13, 30, 34, 35, 38, 159 Marvin Lyons; 18, 32, 43, 45, 53, 74, 77, 95, 106 above, 113, 121, 122, 125, 126, 133, 134, 147, 155, 167, 181 (Schermer Collection), 194, 212 Mansell Collection; 33, 62, 92, 137, 162, 165 Novosti; 28–9, 37, 51, 56, 61 left and right, 66, 80, 85, 88, 91, 98 above and below, 99 above, 107 above, 130, 138, 139 left and right, 142 above, 158, 187, 188–9, 193, 207 Popperfoto; 9, 14, 26, 60, 64, 69, 78, 101, 110, 152, 163, 179, 199, 203 Radio Times Hulton Picture Library; *67* Kenneth Snowman, Wartski; 73 Victoria and Albert Museum; 99 below Roger Viollet; *68* Virginia Museum, Bequest of Lillian Thomas Pratt; endpaper Ullstein; 174 Weidenfeld and Nicolson Archive.

Picture research by Claire Baines.

The author and publisher have taken all possible care in tracing and acknowledging the source and ownership of all illustrations. If any mistakes have accidentally occurred, we shall be pleased to correct them in subsequent editions, provided that we receive notification.

Index

INDEX

INDEX